To Betsy,

Thank you! God Bless!

This Belongs to:
Betsy Baker

The Long Road

A Prodigal's U-Turn to Redemption, Restoration, and Ministry

RANDY KEELING,
WITH BURTON W. COLE

CROSSBOOKS
PUBLISHING

CrossBooks™
A Division of LifeWay
1663 Liberty Drive
Bloomington, IN 47403
www.crossbooks.com
Phone: 1-866-879-0502

In order to protect the identity of emergency personnel and patients, several
of the names have been changed in the EMS sections of the book.

Scripture taken from the King James Version of the Bible.

Scripture quotations taken from the Holy Bible, New Living Translation,
Copyright © 1996, 2004. Used by permission of Tyndale House
Publishers, Inc., Wheaton, Illinois 60189. All rights reserved.

First published by CrossBooks 03/06/2014

ISBN: 978-1-4627-3434-4 (sc)
ISBN: 978-1-4627-3436-8 (hc)
ISBN: 978-1-4627-3435-1 (e)

Library of Congress Control Number: 2014900063

Printed in the United States of America.

This book is printed on acid-free paper.

Acknowledgements

The author wishes to acknowledge the following individuals who have helped in many ways to bring this project to completion.

Kate Hinke. . . . . Manuscript Edit

William Shane Muir. . . . . Manuscript Edit

Terry Cole . . . . Manuscript Edit

Jim Weikal . . . . Manuscript Edit

Emilie Johnston . . . . Manuscript Edit

Jeff Keeling. . . . . Manuscript Edit & Final Edit

Burton W. Cole . . . . Project Assistant

To all of our family, friends, and fans who have prayed for us, loved us, and supported us during the past 20 years of this journey, you have lightened the load and given us much inspiration and encouragement.

To my friend Burton W. Cole who has been by my side throughout this entire journey.

To my Heavenly Father, who knew me from the beginning and who has guided me every step of the way. Thank You!

Dedication

With a heart filled with love and gratitude to the woman who forgave, sacrificed, and showed me what God's unconditional love was about by loving me unconditionally despite the feelings and advice of others. Thanks for never giving up on me and seeing the potential for good that was inside of me. Trish, you truly are a remarkable woman. I love you!

To Jeff, Doug and Lynn, three of the greatest gifts that God has given me, I love you and thank you for never giving up on your father and loving me when I was unlovable. To my daughters-in-law, Hannah and Nancy and my son-in-law, Pat, thank you for being a part of our family. I love you like my own kids. To my grandsons Jacob, Jackson and grandson soon to arrive, I love you so much, you make my life complete.

My prayer for the family is that we will serve God with all our hearts and love each other like there will be no tomorrow. I pray you learn from the mistakes that I made in my life and never duplicate them. But, always remember if you fall along the way, there is a God who loves unconditionally, a God who forgives, a God who restores.

I would also like to dedicate this book to the generations of children who are now in their 30's, 40's, and 50's, who have been hurt greatly by the tragic misrepresentation of holiness. Many of you are still floundering in no-man's land trying figure out where you fit in. I assure you; there is a better way; the only way: one without judgment, criticism and ostracism.

I urge you to forget about what the denominations say and just love the Lord God with all your heart, soul, strength and love your fellow man. Live this way, every day. That's true holiness.

Randy Keeling
October 2013

Contents

Chapter 1   Crossroads 1

Chapter 2   A Shakable Foundation. 3

Chapter 3   Influences 10

Chapter 4   Touched by the Music. 15

Chapter 5   Connie 19

Chapter 6   Trish. 24

Chapter 7   Blood and Bonding. 29

Chapter 8   Close Calls 39

Chapter 9   Despicable Me 44

Chapter 10   A Sweet-Smelling Savor. 51

Chapter 11   Murderous Intent 55

Chapter 12   Forgiven 59

Chapter 13   The Music Begins 65

Chapter 14   Death Route. 74

Chapter 15   Clueless. 81

Chapter 16   Becoming a Dad. 90

Chapter 17   Shaken 98

Chapter 18   Setting a New Course. 104

Chapter 19   The Van's Possessed. 116

Chapter 20   Miracles 123

Chapter 21 Songwriting 132

Chapter 22 Tales from the Road 137

Chapter 23 The Kids. 152

Chapter 24 Family Values 164

Chapter 25 Excuse Me?. 172

Chapter 26 The Last Three Weeks. 180

CHAPTER 1

Crossroads

I t wasn't the fear of hell that propelled me off that bench and crumpled me over the old, wooden altar that Wednesday night. I already lived in a hell of my own making.

My mind raced back to the Sunday night when I stood on the threshold of the door and told my wife, "I don't love you anymore," and tried to explain to my two little boys why Daddy was leaving.

I remembered how, after yet another affair, I sat on the edge of a couch bolstering myself with several drinks. I meant to end a lifetime of pain—but couldn't go through with it. Just another failure in a life full of them.

I'd made many attempts to do the right thing. I'd tried to reconcile with my family. I'd tried to be a good person. But just a few months earlier in a fit of rage, I meant to shoot my father, my wife and kids, then myself. My wife, in desperation, beat me to the truck, where I kept my pistol hidden under the seat, grabbed it and ran down the alley. Otherwise, I have no doubt what the outcome would've been.

As a paramedic, I'd saved many other lives, but I couldn't rescue myself from my own inner despair. From my earliest childhood, all I could remember was insecurity, abuse, suffocating loneliness, anger, fights, and hurt.

A brain abscess took the life of one of my sisters when she was only 17. On emergency calls, I witnessed much trauma. Kids barely younger than I died in my arms. Seeing all the trauma firsthand really messes with your head. I was a wreck.

Many of my EMS partners were just like family. At times, we went through hell together and became very close. Meanwhile, at home, my wife Trish and our three children were that *other* family I had. They couldn't understand my life in emergency services.

Now, on August 18, 1993, my 28th birthday, because of a promise that I had made to my wife—who wouldn't let go of hope, who refused to quit praying—I found myself sitting beside her in an old-fashioned camp meeting service in western Pennsylvania.

I had heard it all before, of course. I grew up in a home where I was bundled off to church every Sunday, Wednesday and revival meeting. If the church doors were open, we were there. From third grade through my senior year, I attended a Christian school that was affiliated with the holiness church we attended. During the course of my youth, I'd been exposed to so many acts of hypocrisy that I thought if this was what God was all about, I'd be better off on my own.

The evangelist preached on the straight and narrow way that evening. I can't tell you the details of what he said. I don't really remember. At one point during the message that Wednesday night, several people in the audience stood and shouted praises to God. One elderly woman was on her feet and twirled her hanky high. God was really there that night, and the air was thick with the presence of the Holy Spirit.

I thought to myself, "Here they are, shouting about this and I'm empty." As this scene unfolded, I realized that what I needed in my life was what they were shouting about.

During the altar call after the message, it was very clear to me that the Lord was saying, "Randy, you need to go forward." I had tried and failed so many times. If I went forward, would this just be another failure? Could I really let go, fully surrender everything to God? In spite of all my fears and doubts that night, I knew I was at a dead end, a one-way street headed for self-destruction. There was no place to run, no place to hide.

I was out of options; something had to change.

CHAPTER 2

A Shakable Foundation

I wish I could tell you my childhood was perfect, but our family, like many others, was extremely dysfunctional in our relationships and our religion.

I was born August 18, 1965, in Worthington, Pennsylvania, the youngest of three children to Dan and Thelma Keeling. My sister Carol was ten and my sister Connie was two.

Dad worked long hours driving a tractor-trailer rig hauling bulk cement. I have many memories of him coming home between eight or nine in the evening, eating dinner, and falling asleep at the table. Mom would wake him and tell him to go to bed, only to see him roll out again at one or two in the morning for the next run.

Dad's birth mother, Bessie, died when Dad was just three days old. His biological father, Loren, couldn't take him in, or perhaps didn't want the responsibility of raising a newborn. Regardless, I believe Dad felt he was responsible for his mother's death in some way. I am certain Dad carried feelings of insecurity and rejection to his grave. At three days old, he was taken in by his aunt and uncle who later adopted him when he was eleven or twelve. Dad's adoptive mother—his own aunt—often told him, "Dan E., remember, you're not my son. You're Bessie's boy." One can only imagine the feelings these words would trigger in the mind of a little boy who longed to have a real family.

Dad often said that his stepsister Margaret was more of a mother to him than his adopted mother, and he loved her dearly. I remember him saying how devastated he was when she left home for Bible college. Dad said his world fell apart because she was the only real stability in his life.

In addition to taking care of our home and us kids, my mother cleaned houses. Mom was a tough woman who grew up in a coal miner's home where fighting was the norm. Mom and her siblings had to be strong, and her family members were known for their size, physical toughness, and mental grit.

Mom has shared many stories with me about the fights that took place in her childhood home. She remembers her dad—my grandfather—grabbing a pipe or an ax in a fit of rage and going after a couple of her brothers and another time when her oldest sister broke their dad's collarbone with a stew pot. Mom and her twin sister Velma would take off running with two of the younger siblings when their parents would fight. They would run, then stop and listen. If they could still hear fighting, they would run again. Throughout the years, I heard many stories—some that were true, and others that may not have been—of the fighting and abuse that took place in the Troup home. All of these events happened before my grandfather, Alvie Troup, became a Christian.

As fate would have it, I took after my mother's side of the family. I would have been a menace on the defensive line of the football team had I attended a public school instead of a private parochial school, which didn't field a team.

As kids, we were raised in church. From as early as I can remember, my parents took us to Sunday school, church, prayer meeting, revival meetings, and camp meetings. If the church doors were open, we were there. From as early as I can remember, most of the emphasis in our religion was placed on our outward appearances. As long as we abided by the rules of the denomination, the condition of our heart relationship with God didn't matter. Or at least it appeared that way. This scenario made it easy for us to look like Christians on the outside. If the tie wasn't black or the sleeves were too short, you were labeled a sinner.

I can remember being at church camp meetings as a small child and hearing the adults saying things like, "Oh my, did you see what they were wearing?" in a whisper, always drawing attention to the outward.

When Samuel was sent to anoint a new king over Israel after God rejected Saul, he was sure that it would be David's older brother because

David's brother looked the part. God told Samuel in 1 Samuel 16:7, "But the Lord said unto Samuel, 'Look not on his countenance, or on the height of his stature; because I have refused him: for the Lord seeth not as a man seeth; for man looketh on the outward appearance, but the Lord looketh on the heart.'" (King James Version)

I believe if Jesus were walking on the earth today, the majority of the mainstream holiness denominations would reject Him and crucify Him again because He may not look and act like the church rulebook says He should.

Like many other families, we had our share of fights. Things generally calmed down around revival meeting time. When a revival meeting came to our church, my sisters and I would try to predict how long our home would stay sane. Usually, we would have about a week of peace, then things would get back to "normal." Dad would say something "wrong," Mom would be upset, and, well…

When I was fourteen, the church we attended was torn apart by a bad split. My dad was on the church board, and my mom also held several offices. Tempers flared even in our home over what was happening at the church. I remember telling my parents, "When I'm on my own, I will never go back to a 'holiness' church. If this is what Christianity is all about, I want nothing to do with it." We were all dressed up looking like saints on the outside, but on the inside, we were—in the words of Jesus—"full of dead men's bones." (Matt. 23:27)

When I say our family fought, I don't mean the occasional yelling matches that happen between most kids and their parents. In my family, fighting meant *fighting*. If you stepped out of line, you'd better look out because you were going to get cuffed alongside the head.

For the most part, my relationship with my mother was somewhat sane. My sisters, Carol and Connie (who is deceased), would no doubt have had their own versions of the story to tell based upon their personal experiences. What I can say from my perspective is that our home life was chaotic. My mother, the rough coal miner's daughter, marrying my father, the insecure adoptee, was a recipe for disaster. I was exposed to many things at home, all under the cover of holiness, to which a child should never be exposed. At this point in the story, I feel it necessary to avoid divulging more of the intimate details. What I can say is that many moments of my childhood were filled with fear, anxiety, emptiness, and despair.

When Dad would do something wrong, he had to face the wrath of Mom. When the preacher did something they didn't agree with, we ate the preacher for Sunday dinner. This would often result in demonstrative reactions that went contrary to Christianity, let alone to a family that looked like the perfect family on Sundays in church.

At home, we had a "do-as-I-say-not-as-I-do" policy. One day, when I was around the age of eight or nine, the neighbor lady made me mad because she wouldn't let her son come out and play. In my anger, I called her a very bad name in front of my sister Connie. As siblings do, my sister told on me. She told my mother, and Mom said, "You wait until your dad gets home."

I cowered in fear all day. When Dad finally did get home, the sparks flew. I was sitting on a lounge chair in the sitting room, and I heard them talking in the kitchen. I knew it was coming, and I was about to get nailed. Dad came into the sitting room, kicked the footrest of the lounge chair down, and jerked me out of my seat. He said, "Get your clothes off." I was forced to strip down to my undershorts. He said, "They gave Jesus thirty-nine stripes. I can give that to you, too."

Dad made me kneel at the bottom of the basement stairs. Then, using his belt, he started from my ankles and worked his way up all the way to my neck. Whenever Dad punished me like this, it was as if he unleashed all his anger and frustrations. I had welts and scabs from where the blood had been drawn during that beating. When Dad said you wouldn't sit down for a week, he meant it.

I remember sleeping on my stomach because it hurt so badly. And Mom made sure I wore a turtleneck to school the next day to cover up the welts and blood marks on my neck, so the damage could be kept hidden. I wish I could say that was the only time I ever got a beating like that, but they happened more often than I care to remember.

Another time, when I was nine or ten years old, Dad came home from work early, so he could do some weeding in the garden. Times were tough, and Mom and Dad always planted a big garden. Each of us kids had chores to do: shelling peas, snapping beans, hoeing and weeding. If you didn't do that right, you were in trouble.

That evening, as Dad weeded, I tossed rocks overtop of the garden. I zipped them way over his head, nowhere close to him. He saw what I was doing and said, "You toss one more rock, and I'm going to knock the living Tarr out of you." Dad made that statement often because his birth name was Dan E. Tarr. When he was adopted, he took on the Keeling name. I have since joked onstage that I'm really glad Dad did so. Otherwise, our singing group might have been known as Randy and the Tarr Babies instead of The Keelings. Thank God for a little bit of humor in the midst of the storm!

Well, you guessed it, I threw one more rock, and Dad, true to his word, stripped me down to my undershorts, and I got it from my ankles to my neck. He was out of control, swinging the leather belt side to side across my naked body. I remember my mom standing at the top of the cellar way because she heard me screaming in pain. "Dan, have a little mercy! Dan, have mercy!" she yelled.

My Dad never did anything the easy way. Due to a lack of finances, Dad did the majority of the home repairs and remodeling projects on his own, squeezing them into whatever spare time he could find. Hiring a backhoe to dig out a basement was never in the plan. Everything was hand-dug with a pick, shovel, and wheelbarrow. I think you get the picture.

One Saturday afternoon, Dad was digging out for a new basement under the sunroom, and he wanted me to "drive the truck"—wheelbarrow duty. It was a beautiful day, and I wanted to play. I guess I wasn't working hard enough or fast enough. Dad became fed up with my whining and grumbling and hauled off and swung the shovel like a ball bat against my backside. I tried to block the shovel with my hand because I knew it was going to hurt. It did. The corner of the shovel caught my left hand nearly cutting off my pinky finger. I still have the scar running across my knuckle.

Eventually, Dad apologized to me about the incident because Mom got on his case pretty hard about what he did. He realized he could have harmed me for life.

The next day was Sunday; we went to church, and I wore bandages on my left hand. Of course, I couldn't tell the truth about the bandages. It all had to be kept hidden, and I lied when somebody would ask me what had happened.

Another time when Mom took my side after a beating involved an incident that occurred on the way home from school when the bus driver made me really mad. Some days she could be royal pain. That particular day, I was really irritated with her, and called her the word for an illegitimate child. Please understand that I learned those words at home.

My big mouth started a chain reaction. The bus driver called my mother; Mother told Dad; and I was toast. When Dad came home, there was no mercy. I was sitting at the kitchen table. Dad yanked off his belt and rapped me alongside the head with the buckle. He caught me on the right temple. Mom quickly got his attention shouting, "You could have killed him!"

Although I went through these experiences as a child, I am still a firm believer in corporal punishment. As an adult, I realize I had done wrong and deserved punishment—but not abuse: never abuse. God created a natural part of the body for correction purposes, and I see nothing wrong with two or three swats on the bottom end to get a child's attention, but discipline is not to be done out of anger or frustration. Before you correct your children, it's always a good idea for you as a parent to take a time-out first.

During my teenage years, Dad was always harping about my hair. "It's too long. Your sideburns are too long." Or God forbid if I got it squared off in the back. He wanted it tapered. I didn't see what the big problem was. It was my head, and I thought my head looked better with a squared cut than a tapered cut. He just couldn't get it.

A couple of times, in his disgust, he ripped his finger across the back of my neck, complaining about yet another haircut. One time, I was so mad I took off and left home, determined not to come back. It seemed as if he always nitpicked over the stupidest things. By this time, Trish and I were dating, and I often used her home as a place of refuge on the weekends.

I know the Bible says we are to honor our father and mother, and I was trying my best; however, kids should have the right to make some tiny decisions about their appearance. I wasn't a robot. One Sunday night Dad got on me again about my hair, which, by the way, was already shorter than ninety percent of the other kids' hair. I was really ticked. What did he expect? Shave my head bald? I wasn't going to take it ever again.

He and I locked arms and went over the bed, and had it not been for Mom breaking us up, I would have done my best to hurt him badly. By now, I was close to six feet tall and weighed 275 pounds. Dad might have been able to lick me, but I was going to give him a run for his money. I was determined never to take his abuse again. I had seen a life of hell; I had taken enough of his abuse; and I wasn't about to change for him or anybody.

CHAPTER 3

Influences

School never offered much refuge from a troubled home, not to mention that I was dealing with a myriad of other issues.

As a boy, I suffered from severe bedwetting. It was so bad that I literally soaked the bed at night. I just couldn't control it. I'd barely get to sleep, and it was as if the Hoover Dam broke loose, and I'd soak the bed again. It probably would have been a good idea for me to keep a rowboat near the side of my bed!

I underwent surgery to stretch my bladder in an attempt to correct the situation. After that, the problem began to subside. After surgery, it occasionally reoccurred, but within a couple years, it went away. My bedwetting problem only added to my already sinking self-esteem.

Another difficulty that I was contending with was dyslexia. Reading has always been hard. Even today, I have to be very careful, especially when reading in public, that I don't add or delete words that are on the page. This is not a good scenario for a man who would one day become a pastor.

When I was in kindergarten, I walked to school. Many times I started out and made it halfway only to return in tears because of fear and insecurity. That was quickly resolved with a trip to Mr. Jones' office—the principal. I realized I feared him more than my other fears.

Then, starting in third grade, I went to a Christian school.

Sometimes parents think sending their kids to a Christian school will shield them from all of the pitfalls often found in public schools. Nothing could be farther from the truth.

In the Christian school, from the administrator's children on down, kids were promiscuous, rebellious, and involved in blatant sin. Kids smoked cigarettes down over the hill from the school during recess. One time, marijuana passed right through my hands to someone else. Pornography was brought to school, and this was all in a so-called "Christian" school.

When I was first introduced to pornography, I was playing at a friend's house. My friend took me under the sun porch of his house and showed me where his brothers stashed their magazines. This opened a whole new world to me, one that would be used later by the devil to wreak havoc in my life.

In the midst of all the insecurities, fears, and anxieties that I had while searching for someone who cared, I found myself grasping for love anywhere I could find it. A void needed to be filled, and pornography was there, warping my thinking, and increasing my appetite to see more. The Bible says in Luke 11:34 that "the lamp of the body is the eye," and what you see with your eyes is recorded on the greatest computer ever created—your brain.

In my adolescence, just like many other kids, my curiosities swirled, but the facts were never explained to me in the proper way. The topic of sex, a natural function of our bodies, was all kept hidden in my family. It was improper to talk about it, and therefore, as a young man, the pornography lit a fire in me that couldn't be put out easily.

The images burned into your mind by pornography are details that the devil will often use to hound you, tempt you, and replay like a video in your thoughts. One of the biggest problems with pornography is you see images of characters engaging in detestable activities, which warps your entire way of thinking about the opposite sex and the concept of sex in general. A common saying is "garbage in, garbage out." Not only are you what you eat, but you also become what you see. There I was, seeing that garbage during the developmental stage of my life, the experimental stage when young kids go through phases such as "show and tell." Looking at pornography warped my thinking and desires, even toward the same sex. The devil was using this tool to draw me in.

As I mentioned, human sexuality was never really explained to me. I learned by hearsay. I constantly heard things from other kids, and I was curious because I didn't know what they were talking about. Curiosity kills the cat as they say, and because I didn't have the proper nurturing at home,

I was attracted toward anyone who showed me affection. Many kids even of the same sex will engage in "show and tell," but that was not for me. I was attracted to the opposite sex.

Throughout my teenage years, any time I had the opportunity to view pornography, I was ready and willing to look. If there was an opportunity to be intimate with a girl, I was there. Always learning, always exploring, I craved affection. I needed it, and the more I got, the more I wanted. I also wasn't doing well academically. At my school, there were individuals who barely had gone to college themselves attempting to be teachers. Some had not graduated from college, and others had only majored in Bible courses, but now they were trying to teach algebra, geometry, trigonometry, biology, and advanced science. It was not a good scenario. Granted, there were a small handful of teachers who had graduated not only from Bible college but had received additional degrees from secular colleges. This, however, was not the norm.

One event that rocked my world in high school had nothing to do with academics. I needed a role model, and there was a school administrator in whom I had a great deal of confidence. I looked up to him and wanted to believe in him. One day during a revival meeting, the administrator made a public confession in chapel service that he had not been living as a Christian should be living. That shook my foundations.

Now that I'm a Christian, I understand that sometimes even the best of us can fall. Today, I enjoy a friendship with that former administrator, but during the time when I really needed stability and a hero, hearing his public confession knocked me for a loop.

But it is not God's way to leave us without examples, and there were some wonderful models of His grace during my childhood. Two people whom I dearly loved attended our church in NuMine, Pennsylvania: Carl and Jean McIntyre. Jean was my aunt through marriage, sort of like a step-aunt. As I look back into my childhood, I can truly say Uncle Carl and Aunt Jean are two people I miss.

Aunt Jean could tell wonderful stories. After church, we would gather tightly around her. "Hey, Aunt Jean, tell us a story, tell us a story!" And she would tell some of the things that happened to her when she was a little girl. She talked about the funny things and the scary things, like the time while she was in bed and the piano in their living room began to play. She thought the house was haunted. It could have been the cat, but she didn't get up to find out. We'll probably never know the real truth to the story. But it was fun, and she could entertain us for hours.

Carl and Jean were gentle people, and when Aunt Jean hugged you, you felt warm all over. You knew by her touch that she loved you, and you wanted to latch onto her and stay with her forever. Uncle Carl was also that way, gentle and mild-mannered, and when he laid his hand on your shoulder, you knew he cared about you. They were, in my description, genuine Christians. Not only did they talk the talk, but they walked the walk and lived what they believed.

Another lady in that church who stood out to me was Ethel Eicher. She was blind, and my family would often pick her up and give her a ride to church. Every year, Ethel would get up during the Christmas program and read the Christmas story from her Braille Bible. I would watch, completely fascinated as her fingers ran across the page deciphering the Braille letters.

In spite of her blindness, we couldn't confuse Ethel's sense of direction. Many Sundays after church, we kids had fun taking Ethel outside in front of the church, where we spun her in circles, and when we stopped, we'd say, "Okay, Ethel, point to the east," and she always pointed east. And we'd spin her around again and say, "Okay, point to the south," and she pointed to the south. We could never trick her. It was amazing to see her in action. I really miss Ethel.

For a couple of summers and some evenings during high school, I worked for Rich and Iona Brocious on their farm. I hold fond memories of my time working for them. On the farm, I felt free. Mr. and Mrs. Brocious were hard-working people who always treated me well.

At any given time, Mr. Brocious kept approximately 800 chickens, 300 head of hogs and about 22 head of beef cattle. He also raised corn, oats and the other crops farmers usually grow. I loved raking and baling hay and operating the machinery. Gathering eggs was okay until one of the old biddies would develop an attitude and wouldn't let me take the egg from under her, and I would get pecked. But as for cleaning the pigpens and chicken coops, which I did often—someone else can take care of that!

I always appreciated the Brocious's kindness. Although there were some days I probably didn't work as hard as I should have, they were always there for me either to talk or provide a listening ear. Mrs. Brocious was a great cook and made terrific Dagwood sandwiches stacked high with fried eggs, ham or bacon, cheese, lettuce, tomato, and onion.

I had many good times growing up, but they were often overshadowed by the bad. When I reflect upon my childhood, the majority of it is a thick, black cloud.

CHAPTER 4

Touched by the Music

In spite of a chaotic childhood, music broke through. I didn't know it then, but God was planting a passion for Gospel music within me and preparing me for what eventually would become a successful music ministry and church pastorate.

At home we had an old RCA record player with attached speakers. One evening when I was about two years old, I was lying on the dining room floor listening to a stack of old 33-rpm vinyl LPs of Gospel music. I heard the song *How Great Thou Art,* and I began to cry. As a little boy, I didn't have the words to explain the emotions, but I'll never forget what I felt. All I knew was that the music moved me, and it was as if God hovered right there speaking to a little boy's heart.

I remember walking into the kitchen weeping and my mother asking, "Randy, what's the matter?" She thought I'd hurt myself, but I wasn't injured. Then it dawned on her that I was hearing the music, and it was affecting me. I can't recall the name of the recording artist who was singing on the album, but God used it to touch my heart. If there's an insect known as the Gospel music bug, I got bit, and the effects would last a lifetime.

Some of the better memories of my childhood came from gathering around the piano to sing. Mom, my sisters, and I spent many evenings singing songs out of the old *Praise and Worship* hymnal since we never had a television.

Mom taught me how to sing the women's alto part, which is the male baritone part an octave higher. I also learned the tenor part. I could sing lead, and although my voice wasn't exceptionally low, I could hear the bass part. Mom was a major factor in teaching me how to sing four-part harmony and how to pick up tunes by ear. I have since discovered that God has given me a natural gift. When I write a song, I write it in four-part harmony, hearing all parts at the same time. On occasions when Dad came home from work early, he would join the ensemble. Mostly, he would sing the lead, and sometimes he sang tenor. These were the best times at home.

My mother learned to play the piano at a very young age, and with just a handful of lessons, she played quite well. One of the things we enjoyed was covering mom's eyes or putting a blindfold on her and having her play by ear. I have teased that she played by ear so much that her ears now look funny. Neater than that was when we could coax her to transpose music into different keys blindfolded. We were never disappointed; Mom could do it with ease.

For more than fifty years, Mom has been the church pianist in every church she has attended. She, like me, also has the ability to hear all the harmony parts, something that apparently runs in the bloodline of her family.

My first public performance came at the age of two when I was asked to sing at the small, country church we attended for the Christmas program. I sang "Silent Night," and recited a lengthy selection called *Happy Birthday, Jesus*. It was quite an effort for a child of two, but Mom made sure I did it very well, rehearsing with me for hours. The people at church often commented on the way in which I put all the expression and emotion into the recitation. My mother drilled that into me as well. She wanted her kids to look good in front of people. And furthermore, I was too young to be scared.

I took piano lessons for more than five years, beginning in elementary school and continuing on into junior high. Mother made sure that we didn't waste her hard-earned money ensuring that we practiced every day. Failure to practice was a crime, and you didn't want to get crossways with Mom. She knew if you were playing it right and would quickly be there to correct you if it was wrong.

The coordination in my left hand has never been great. When I try to play the piano, my right and left hands refuse to work together. It was in these moments that my nervous twitches and habits were more prevalent. The stress of playing coupled with the stress of a troubled home didn't help.

In spite of it all, I still managed to learn some things about music and loved it. In addition to piano lessons, I also learned to play the trumpet. With that, I didn't have to worry about my left hand not working. All I needed was the right. I also took voice lessons, and after I was married, I took more piano lessons, a year of drum lessons and conducting lessons.

When I was seven years old, Mom and Dad bought me my first horn. I'll never forget the day we journeyed to Johnny Murphy Music in Leechburg, Pennsylvania, about twenty-five miles from home to make the purchase. It was a Holton beginner model. It was gold in color and was definitely used but in good shape. They paid $95 for it, and I still own it today.

Shortly after receiving the instrument, I began taking trumpet lessons from the band director at Redbank Valley High School in New Bethlehem, Pennsylvania. Although I only took about a year and a half of trumpet lessons, I possessed a natural ability to play by ear, which interfered greatly with my motivation to read sheet music.

When trumpet lessons ended, I embarked on a fifteen-year trek of continuing to play every day, in some cases for hours. One year, I got a collection of marches and played along with them—"Under the Double Eagle," "The Stars and Stripes Forever," and "America Forever." I trumpeted along with the Kittanning Firemen's band, a local marching unit that recorded an album. I loved the Silver Chords, and Danny Davis and the Nashville Brass. I played along with their records over and over again and just about drove Mom and Dad nuts. I even started to blast along with some pop tunes of the day that featured brass. I was a great fan of the pop group Chicago, and I even tried playing along with the Bee Gees on "Stayin' Alive."

I played the trumpet often in those days in high school orchestra, church, and during school events and became quite accomplished. Not a professional, but not too shabby either.

Gospel music was always my first love. It moved me in ways that other music didn't. I enjoyed listening to groups like The Cathedrals, the Statesmen, the Blackwood Brothers, and the Blue Ridge Quartet. I loved hymns, quartet-style singing, and orchestrated music.

My dad was a big fan of opera-style singing. One of Dad's favorite singers was Jerome Hines, a famous operatic bass. Had it not been for my dad's insecurities, and if he'd had proper encouragement, he could have been a great singer. Deep inside, I knew he would have liked to study opera. Whether shifting gears in a truck or singing, he often approached these two subjects from a scientific point of view. We often heard him practicing his singing in the basement or in the shower. It drove my mother nuts! At the time, we kids made fun of him. But with some coaching and proper training, Dad could have been great.

I, on the other hand, had eclectic tastes. Although Gospel music was my favorite, I'd get the hankering to listen to Styx, Journey, Foreigner, REO Speedwagon, Earth, Wind & Fire, Little River Band, Survivor, and a little bit of country. My sister Carol listened to Karen Carpenter, Charlie Pride, Neil Diamond, Alabama, and the Oak Ridge Boys. I didn't mind them either. On occasion, we traveled to Pittsburgh to hear the Pittsburgh Symphony in concert at Heinz Hall. That was a treat. On Saturday evenings, I'd be listening to classical music on WQED, and on Sunday nights after church I was listening to Burt Jones playing hymns on the organ on WPIT. I listened to everything. I just loved music.

I never had much trouble singing out loud or in public. My wife tells me often that I have a built-in microphone. She's right.

Mom and Dad didn't have high hopes that I'd make anything of myself in the music industry. But being bullheaded and stubborn, I had to forge ahead in my own way.

CHAPTER 5

Connie

Connie was 17, and I was 15. From the third grade on, she and I waited for and rode the bus to school together every day. She was a great alto singer, and she also played clarinet in the school orchestra.

Connie and I used to fight. Oh man, we used to get angry at each other! She'd never budge or bend or bow for any reason if she thought she was right. And if she got hold of you, she'd claw you like a cat. Put it this way, if you got near her, you were going to get nailed. I'm sure I was a pest and did my share of tormenting and teasing, and probably deserved most of what I got. Brothers and sisters usually never get along all the time, but in the end, they'll stick up for each other if someone other than their sibling comes after them.

One Monday afternoon during choir practice in her senior year in 1981, I saw her reach up and grab the back of her head, and her face turned a ghastly white. She was in terrific pain and nauseated. It was all she could do to ride home on the bus with me and walk up the hill to our house. Little did we know that would be her last day to attend school.

Mom and Dad didn't know what to do. Connie was so sick, and all she wanted to do was lie on the couch. She could barely raise her head. Connie complained of a terrible headache. She couldn't eat and continued to be severely nauseated.

First, Mom and Dad took Connie to the emergency room at Kittanning Hospital, only to be sent home with a diagnosis of the flu. Through the rest of that week, her condition worsened, and Mom and Dad thought a trip to the chiropractor might help because something might be out of place in her back or neck. Connie was prone to vertebrae slipping out of place.

On the Sunday afternoon when Mom and Dad took Connie to the chiropractor, I took a walk to the playground at the old school where I had attended kindergarten. I was alone, and I still remember how beautiful the sky looked as I laid on my back in the field. One of those picture-perfect days: white puffy clouds, blue sky, and sunshine.

With my eyes closed, relaxing, I saw it—a vision of my sister Connie, lying in a casket. In my mind's eye, I saw her hair draped—she had long, beautiful hair—and it was flowing around both sides of her face. She was wearing a white dress. The thought immediately came to me: "My sister's going to die."

After this premonition, I got up and went home, walking down the hill, retracing those steps I had walked so many times when I was going to kindergarten. My older sister, Carol, met me at the door. "Where were you? I was worried about you."

Mom and Dad had left earlier that day to take Connie to the doctor. She had been sick for the previous week. Carol and my brother-in-law Paul had come for a visit, and Carol was to keep an eye on me. I told her I'd been up at the school playground just relaxing in the field.

Then, I told Carol, "Connie's going to die. I just saw a picture of her in my mind, lying in a casket."

Carol started to cry. "Don't talk like that! Don't say those things!"

Call it a dream; call it a vision; call it a premonition; regardless, I saw her, and there was no doubt about what I saw.

During the following week, Mom and Dad took Connie back to the emergency room in Kittanning where she was referred to a neurologist at Butler Memorial Hospital for the following Monday. After the visit to the neurologist, she was scheduled for brain surgery at North Hills Passavant Hospital in Pittsburgh. In preparation for surgery, the medical staff had to shave her head. Connie's long, beautiful hair had to be removed. I remember the nurses taking great care to save her hair for possible use later.

At the end of her surgery, Connie slipped into respiratory and cardiac arrest in the recovery room. I'll never forget when the doctor told us what was happening and that they were trying to get her vital signs and stabilize her. They wanted to know if there was anything in our family history that had been overlooked.

We didn't know it at the time, but Connie had been born with a congenital heart defect. The right side of her heart was enlarged to twice the size of the left side, and she had been struggling for years. There were also holes in her heart. This information was never discovered until after the surgery. In the second grade, Connie had gone through a bout of double pneumonia. They thought she was going to die then. But somehow, miraculously, she survived. She seemed fine, and amazingly, she was a strong girl.

We learned that Connie had a brain abscess, almost like a tumor, that was inter-related with the heart condition we knew nothing about. The doctors literally brought her back from the brink of death in the recovery room, to a point at which she was able to live out the rest of that week. We were able to talk to her as she was coherent. The brain surgery was successful; however, heart disease took her life. Connie's heart was too weak to handle the surgery, and the medications and stress only complicated matters. In retrospect, the doctor said if they had performed heart surgery first, then taken care of the brain, she might have survived.

Two weeks to the day from when I had the premonition about her death, we walked into Bly Funeral Home in Dayton, Pennsylvania, on Easter Sunday 1981 to view Connie's body. The funeral director had taken Connie's cut hair that had been saved from the hospital, and used it to make my sister look as natural as possible. What I saw in reality on that Easter Sunday looked exactly like what I had seen in my mind's eye only two weeks earlier, white dress and all.

Every cloud is silver-lined. The good part of Connie's story happened on the Sunday night before the Monday when she became ill. Connie went forward that night and accepted Christ as her savior at an altar call during a revival meeting at the church we attended in Templeton, Pennsylvania.

At the end of the altar service, the custom was to have a testimony meeting, and new converts were given the opportunity to share what God had just done for them. That night, my sister stood behind me and gave a resounding testimony of God's saving grace and told how her life had just been changed. During her testimony, she placed her hands on my shoulders and said, "I am now praying that my brother will get saved, also."

The memory of feeling her hands on my shoulders and hearing the words that she said used to be a haunting memory. But today, since my life has been changed, it is a great memory.

I thank God for the opportunity to see my sister the night before she died. That Thursday evening I had a few minutes alone with Connie in the intensive care room. I remember the turban she wore on her head, and I remember holding a Popsicle for her to lick. I told her that night that I loved her, and I was sorry for being mean and all the times that I fought with her. Connie could hardly respond but she was able to squeeze my hand. I would say, "If you can hear me, if you can understand, squeeze my hand," and she squeezed my hand every time.

Looking back, I thank the Lord for the opportunity I had to make things right with Connie. I am thankful that I don't carry the guilt of unsaid words.

The next afternoon, Good Friday, the family went to the hospital cafeteria for lunch. As we stepped off the elevator returning from lunch, a nurse met us with the news that Connie had passed away.

I'll never forget the screams and wailing from Mom and Carol. I remember my mother gritting her teeth, and the groans coming from her were like nothing I'd ever heard before, groaning that was coming from the innermost part of her soul. Carol and my mother were barely able to stand. The grief was almost more than they could bear. Dad just shook convulsively, tears streaming down his face. Those scenes and sounds made an indelible impression. To this day, thirty-three years later, I can still feel the emotion of the moment.

The question my sister Carol struggled with was did Connie make it to Heaven or was she in Hell? I never doubted for a moment she was in Heaven because I was there the night she was saved and heard her testimony. Carol wasn't there to observe the events that had happened on that Sunday night, so she naturally struggled with this question. But God answered the question for her in a beautiful way. Some weeks later, in a dream she saw a man with beautiful, snow-white hair and piercing eyes. His arms were outstretched and lying in them was our sister Connie.

Appropriately, the phrase inscribed on my sister's tombstone is "Safe in the arms of Jesus."

After Connie's death, things changed drastically. The dysfunction in our home began to subside, and all was definitely quieter. In some way, I would like to believe that the healing process was initiated in our home. They say that everything happens for a reason, and I believe that God used this tragedy to begin the restoration process.

CHAPTER 6

Trish

One of the greatest moments in my life happened when I met Trish.

One of my family's annual traditions was to attend church camp in Stoneboro, Pennsylvania. We usually attended camp three times every summer—conference in June, youth camp in July, and family camp in August.

During family camp in 1978, my twelve-year-old cousin and I sat together during services. On this particular night, I remember looking at the opposite end of the pew, and there she was—pretty, petite, a very fine specimen of womanhood! She was sitting with her cousin that night, and although I attempted to listen to the sermon, I remained quite distracted. I couldn't keep my eyes off her.

Archie Atwell, the evangelist, preached about running the good race. He told a story about the time he rode in a bicycle race while serving in the U.S. military. Rev. Atwell's storytelling was hilarious, and the meeting erupted with laughter. I stole more glances at the girl. She was enjoying the story as well. My eyes just kept wandering in her direction.

Archie described the race and his buddies cheering him on: "C'mon, Atwell! C'mon, Atwell!" Then just before he made it to the finish line, he hit a chuckhole, flew over the handlebars and landed in a heap. He jumped back on his bicycle, pedaled like crazy, and won the race—only to receive the prize of a Three Musketeers candy bar.

After the service ended, tradition demanded that if you spotted a good-looking girl, the cool thing to do was ask her to walk on the paved road that circles throughout the campground. Stoneboro camp was no small place. On many Sundays during family camp, there would be as many as 5,000 people on the grounds, which made it a great place to meet girls. Through the week, for something special, you could take her to the candy store, which was the hot spot to hang out and, for seventy-five cents, purchase your date a Steese's old-fashioned Nutty Buddy or banana Popsicle.

As you may have already assumed, I made a beeline to find that girl and ask her if she would walk with me. She said, "Yes."

As we walked, I found out her name was Trish, and about the second or third time around the block, I finally got up the nerve to ask her how old she was. Seventeen! I didn't believe her. She pulled out her driver's license to prove her age. I was only *thirteen,* and right then and there wanted to be like the Tasmanian Devil and bore a hole down through the pavement and disappear. I was always big for my age, and in 1978 I probably was close to 5-foot-10 and about 270 pounds. I was always a big dude. I'm not sure what Trish was thinking when she met me but she kept walking with me.

I really took a liking to her, and she and I became good friends. We spent time together when camp was in session for the next several years. She was a person I looked forward to talking to every year. I could tell her anything, and we had an open line of communication. She was *that* somebody who I could trust. Out of everyone I'd ever been around, she was a straight-shooter, a gem with very strong convictions. Trish was a solid Christian and attempted to do things the right way.

During the next few years, our relationship developed into something that was deep and genuine. *Finally,* I turned sixteen and got my driver's license. Now, I could officially ask her out on a date. This would now make her *twenty,* and yes, there were several other guys vying for her attention. But I won—without having to get physical.

Our first date was to the Cranberry Mall near Franklin, Pennsylvania. Trish wouldn't let me buy her anything other than a drink, and all we did was sit in the lounge in the mall commons and talk. Trish was the kind of girl who never required anything special to make her happy. I found out that she was just happy to be with me. For whatever reason, she saw something in me she liked, and it was great to be with her.

On the last night of Stoneboro camp in 1981, out in the old parking lot near Dorm 120, we had our first kiss, right there on the church campgrounds. I'm not afraid to tell that—now! I'll never forget that night as she softly whispered the words, "I love you."

"Did I hear you right? Did I just hear what I think I heard you say?" And she said, "Yes."

I immediately embraced her and said, "I love you, too." And thus began what we have today.

Over the next several years, our relationship continued to grow. And soon, I popped the question: "Will you marry me?" And she said, "Yes."

We were in her driveway after coming back from a date, sitting in my old 1972 Grand Coupe Plymouth Fury, the pride and joy of my life at that time—as far as vehicles were concerned. The old Grand Coupe had a 318 V8 engine with a high-speed police rear end in it. I could do ninety-five miles per hour in second gear. My dad never believed me until I proved it to him. It's a wonder I didn't kill myself with that car. By today's standards, the Fury was a big ol' boat, about as big as the Titanic.

By now, Trish and I were really tight. We just knew that it was time and were spending every weekend together. I worked as a night stock clerk at the McKean Street Shop 'N' Save grocery store in Kittanning, Pennsylvania through my high school years. I worked a shift on Saturday, usually 6:00 a.m. to 2:00 p.m., and after work, I would jump in the old Plymouth and head north. I would stay overnight at her place with her family, go to church with them on Sundays, and on Sunday nights, head back to my home in Worthington, about seventy miles away.

(By the way, I got my first speeding ticket on the way home from her place at the age of seventeen, doing sixty-five in a fifty-five-miles-per-hour zone near Prospect, Pennsylvania. I wasn't a happy camper. Neither were Mom and Dad.)

At the time I proposed to Trish, in my mind I was totally confused, messed up and warped, but I could not tell her. I knew I loved her, but I couldn't really explain to her how I was feeling inside. I had learned well how to disguise my emotions. Deep in the darkest places of my soul lived frustration, hurt, emptiness, and anxiety. Yet I loved her, and God knew that I would need a strong woman—a woman of great integrity—in my life. One of things I loved about Trish was her ability to lend a listening ear, so I could unload my feelings.

What I really needed most, but was too blind to see, was the healing, fulfillment, and satisfaction that could only come from a relationship with a loving God.

Although I wouldn't admit it to most people, I felt in my heart that someday God might call me into full-time ministry that could involve music. The night I proposed to Trish, in addition to asking her if she would marry me, I also asked her, "If God calls me into a music ministry, will you go with me?" She said "yes" to that question as well, and from that day to this, she has kept her word and has stood faithfully by my side every step of the way.

We married on May 18, 1984. It was a Friday night, and when I think about it, it seems surreal. It's hard to believe that it all happened. We were married at the Wildcat Wesleyan Methodist Church in Rimersburg, Pennsylvania. It wasn't a fancy wedding, but it was just right.

Just about now you're probably wondering how in the world did a church get a name like Wildcat? Down deep in the heart of southern Clarion County in football player Jim Kelly country near East Brady, Pennsylvania, there's the small town of Rimersburg, a town made up of hard-working coal miners and home to the famous Archway Cookies factory. Wildcats once roamed the hills on the outskirts of town, which is how the church there got its name.

As we walked out of the church after the ceremony, somebody whipped a whole handful of rice at us. I took the brunt of it on the left side of my face. As a result, you can see red welts on my face in our wedding photos.

After the reception, we headed out. First, we went to one of my favorite places on earth, Gettysburg, Pennsylvania. Then after a short visit back to our apartment in Worthington, we headed out again for a couple days at Niagara Falls.

When I got married, I was quite naïve. I was as green as the grass. I graduated from high school at age seventeen and got married when I was eighteen which, in retrospect, was way too early. I was young and unprepared to face the challenges that would soon be coming. Nevertheless, I was married, and within that first year, our first son, Jeffrey, was born.

I was nineteen years old with hardly any income, no vision for the future, and a major case of mixed up priorities. Now, I had my first major responsibility, a brand new son. It was like a ball bat smacking me alongside the head. I remember thinking, "Oh man, what did I just do?" I knew it was time to grow up, to be a husband, a dad, a provider. It was time to step up, but I wasn't ready. I had never been properly trained.

And the worst was yet to come.

CHAPTER 7

Blood and Bonding

I don't remember what age I was other than it was prior to kindergarten. I was walking with my mother near Henry's Market, a grocery store on Main Street in Worthington. As we walked away from the market, I heard something that captivated my attention—the fire siren from our local volunteer fire department had begun to wail.

I'll never forget hearing the siren and watching the volunteers run toward the station. Within minutes, the old 1962 pumper roared past us with lights blazing and sirens wailing and several firefighters clinging to the handrail on the back of the truck. From that moment on, I wanted to be near the action.

I loved fire trucks and ambulances so much that when I was a young boy, Mom and Dad purchased several Matchbox and Tonka rescue vehicles for me to use to exercise my imagination. They bought me a pedal fire engine that had its own ladders, hose, and lights that worked. I was in my glory. I was the hero! Often at night, I would entertain myself with books like "The Fire Cat," about Pickles who lived in a firehouse.

When I was fourteen, I became a junior firefighter with the Worthington West Franklin Volunteer Fire Department. Wow! I had finally made it—or so I thought. I had my very own red fire helmet, and I was gung-ho, very eager to test my knowledge in the fire service. I was allowed to be a grunt on the fire ground, but due to my age, I was not yet allowed to ride on the trucks. I had to wait for the second milestone, my sixteenth birthday.

Finally, on the day I turned sixteen, I graduated to a black fire helmet, and I was able to ride on the engine. To my delight, I was rewarded on my sixteenth birthday with a ride on the back of the fire truck with all the other guys to a brush and grass fire out in the country. I was big stuff, running through the fields with an Indian Can—a five-gallon metal can with a small hose and nozzle—strapped to my back, putting out the brush fire! It was *awesome*.

Along with being a junior firefighter, I started into the emergency medical service field when I was a junior in high school. Two things inspired me: a CPR (cardiopulmonary resuscitation) class that was given at our high school, and the unfortunate reading of my sister's autopsy report after her death. I needed to know more. The instructor of my first CPR class said I was a natural, and I should think about pursuing a career in emergency services.

My first ambulance call happened late one evening at the home of one of our neighbors at the bottom of Property Hill. I heard the call on the scanner and made it to her house at the same time the ambulance did. Our neighbor had experienced a massive stroke and as a result was in full cardiac arrest. Having been recently certified in the techniques of CPR—I hate to admit this, but it was to my delight—I was invited to assist the EMTs in performing CPR procedures and transporting her to the hospital.

By now, I was hooked, and in the coming years, I used a variety of excuses to occasionally skip school, and one of those was emergency calls. The teachers would be understanding and let me go.

I'll never forget one morning when our department was called to assist the South Buffalo Township Fire Department with a major structure fire at a chemical plant, a facility that combined various types of fuel sources—such as jet fuel, diesel and gasoline—to make better grades of fuel. I was on one of the first engines to the scene, and when we arrived, the plant was fully involved. All we could do was what we call "surround and drown."

It was one of the most spectacular fires I've ever laid eyes on. Fifty-five gallon drums of fuel would explode and shoot like bullets straight into the air, with a plume of smoke behind them. We had to keep backing up our perimeter, and all we could do was hit it with two-and-a-half-inch hose lines. In fact, my cousin Ron Miller, who lived at least five miles away from the scene of the fire, saw the barrels exploding into the air and could see the plumes of smoke from his house. I will always remember that day.

Due to my size and strength and the fact that I was already certified in CPR, I began responding with our volunteer ambulance service on a regular basis. Immediately following high school, I enrolled at Butler Community College to begin my training to become an emergency medical technician (EMT). After my training, in addition to my duties with the fire department, I routinely responded on emergency ambulance calls. This practice continued through the first few months of my marriage to Trish. When the Shop 'N' Save grocery store where I had been working nights closed, Trish suggested that I should check into taking a job as a professional EMT.

In early September 1984, we made the trip to Trish's former home in Hadley. She had told me that the nearby town of Greenville, Pennsylvania, had a paid ambulance service that might be hiring certified EMTs.

I walked into the office of Gold Cross Ambulance for the first time and met Fred, the manager. He asked to see my CPR and EMT certifications and my driver's license which I readily provided. He gave me an application, said they were hiring and that he would be willing to hire me. He told me to fill out the application and bring it to the office next week and he would put me on the schedule. Wow! I had finally made it to the big time. I was going to be a professional EMT.

In the EMS world, we always had a joke that went something like this: "I used to be hungry and out of work, but then I went to EMT school and now I are one."

When the next week finally came, I walked back into that same office only to find that Fred wasn't there anymore. The new manager, Joe, asked, "And who are you?" I said, "My name is Randy Keeling. Fred hired me last week, and I was told to come back today to turn in my application, and he would put me on the schedule." Joe's reply was, "Well, Fred did a lot of things we didn't know about."

I didn't know it at the time, but found out later that Fred had been embezzling money from the company to the tune of several thousand dollars.

Joe basically put me through the whole rigmarole again and asked how soon I would be available to work. My reply was, "How about tomorrow?"

At 7:00 a.m. the next morning, I was on my first 24-hour tour of duty with my first partner, Steve. And shortly after 7:00 a.m., Car 411, the unit I was assigned to, was responding to Riley Road, Greenville, for a lady in full cardiac arrest as a result of choking on a large marshmallow. Unfortunately, she did not make it. I had just been baptized into the world of professional EMS.

During my first several years at Gold Cross, I did anything and everything I was asked to do. If they needed me to work an extra 12-hour shift, I did it. If they needed me to do a body removal, I did that. If they needed me for on-call duty, I never said, "No." Times were hard; we needed the money; and I was willing to stand on my head or bend over backward to accommodate.

I'll never forget some of the calls we responded to.

One incident that comes to mind involved a young girl, a high school senior, who died as the result of a tragic motor vehicle accident at the intersection of Route 18 and Wasser Bridge Road. She and some of her friends had just left Reynolds High School and were traveling at a high rate of speed. The car crashed, and she was thrown from the vehicle. The memory of seeing her body lying lifeless on the road and then transporting her to the morgue is burned permanently in my mind. She was only seventeen.

Then there was Cliff Williams, one of only three saves that I had as a result of resuscitative efforts. We were called to respond to the old Folk Drugstore in downtown Greenville. When we arrived, he was sitting upright in a chair in full cardiac arrest. My partner Jane and I, along with the help of a nurse who happened to be at the scene, started CPR on Cliff. This was before the days of paramedics in Mercer County. No advanced life support was available. The only thing we could do is what we called "thump and pump" on his chest and provide oxygen.

No sooner did we get him to the ER than he was back with the living. He gave a gasp, his eyes fluttered open and that was that, a successful save. That was an awesome feeling knowing that we had just been a part of saving someone's life.

The irony of it is that three weeks later, Jane and I were called to Cliff's residence in Greenville, where we found him sitting upright on the couch. He'd been deceased for the better part of a day.

One night while working with Steve, we were called to respond to a motor vehicle accident at the top of West Main hill in Greenville. The intoxicated driver of a van, ran off the road and hit a series of trees, then crashed head-on into a telephone pole. The irony of this accident was that the fellow who was driving was not severely hurt, but his passenger, who had not had so much as a drop of alcohol, was in a world of hurt.

When we arrived on scene, it was obvious that the front of the van was trashed. Firefighters were using the Jaws of Life hydraulic cutting tool in an attempt to free the victims from the wreckage. My partner Steve and I were able to open the back doors of the panel van which allowed us to gain access to our patient, the passenger.

I was probably twenty-one at this time, and this was one incident that God really used to remind me that I was lost and in need of Him. I don't remember our patient's name, but I'll never forget his face. Nor will I ever forget the words that he said to me.

He lay diagonally with his legs entangled in the right front side of the van. His head and part of his shoulders rested on the floor behind the driver's seat. The other guy, who had been drinking and driving, was fine, but he was pinned across the chest of our patient. There was no doubt that the driver would survive, so Steve and I left him to the care of other EMTs and focused our attention on the passenger. He was in bad shape.

Steve and I did the best we could to stop the bleeding and to administer high-flow oxygen. While all this was all going on, in the background we heard breaking glass and crunching metal due to the force of the Jaws of Life. They worked feverishly to free our patient. We were unable to immobilize our patient properly until he was disentangled. But as we had done so many times before in situations like this, we tried to stabilize him. I had hold of his hand and tried to reassure him that everything would be okay. His face was a ghostly white color, and it was obvious that he was in hypovolemic shock due to severe blood loss; his heart simply couldn't pump enough blood to the rest of his body.

In those moments that seemed like hours, he looked at me and said, "Am I going to die?"

These are the things that you never learn in training. These are the times that you throw out the manual. I knew in my heart that he was never going to make it. They say you should never lie to your patient. But that day, all I could say was, "Man, I don't know, but I'm here, and we're going to do everything we can do to save your life."

While they worked to free his legs, I kept holding onto his hands and I said, "I'm not going to let you go. I'm here, I'm here, just stay with me."

When they finally cut away enough of the vehicle so they could lift the other guy off his chest it was like somebody pulled the plug. Just like that, he slipped away into eternity. We found out later that he died instantly when the pressure of the other man was removed from his chest. He'd had a complete transection of the aorta, and superior and inferior vena cava veins.

God definitely used this incident to remind me that if something were to happen to me, I was not ready to die. Scarier yet were the number of times I nearly did die, the times I should have been killed. Except for the mercy of an awesome God, I shouldn't be alive to tell this story today.

When we knew that advanced life support (ALS) would be coming to our county, I went on to paramedic training at Clarion Hospital. During that time, I continued to work my regular shifts on the ambulance and also began working in our communications center in Struthers, Ohio as a dispatcher. Remember, I needed the money. I was willing to do anything.

The communications center was a hectic place, as we dispatched some fifty EMS units covering 3,000 square miles of area from Alliance, Ohio, to Grove City, Pennsylvania. Additionally, we dispatched for the Coitsville and Poland Township fire departments in Ohio. Needless to say, there were some days you would come out of the communications center with less hair than what you went in with.

The day finally came that I passed my state boards. I was a full-fledged paramedic. And a couple of years later, I ended up as one of four paramedic supervisors for Gold Cross in Mercer County, Pennsylvania. I loved EMS. I couldn't get enough of it.

One night in Fredonia, Pennsylvania, we got called for a possible attempted suicide. When we arrived on scene, we found this guy sitting on the second-story window ledge, threatening to jump. Although I was a brand new paramedic, I was still seasoned in my approach to patients and wasn't afraid to interact with them.

He kept saying, "I'm going to jump. Don't come any further. I'm going to jump." I kept trying to talk him back into the room, but he wouldn't budge. In my frustration, I decided to take a new approach, another one of those things you don't learn in the textbook.

"Okay, you want to jump, go ahead. Go ahead and jump. You'll be easier to get to when you're on the ground. And furthermore, I won't have to carry your backside down two flights of stairs." What did I care if he broke his leg? He would still be easier to handle from the ground.

Whether as a result of my new tactics or a change in the weather, we finally talked him into going to the hospital with us. He was disgruntled because his girlfriend had broken up with him. He showed me his arms—slash marks ran all up and down them. "I didn't have a knife sharp enough," he said. He was having a very bad day.

We loaded him onto the stretcher and headed to the hospital. My partner Shelly drove and I sat in the back with this guy. I told him we were going to take him to talk to the doctor for an evaluation and maybe some psychological help. On the way in, this crazy dude reached into the inside pocket of his jean jacket and pulled out yet another knife! "You know what, I'm just going to do it." And he starts acting like he's going to cut his arm again.

I went ballistic. I grabbed him, got the knife away from him, and jumped on him with all fours, and hollered at him, "Don't you *ever* do that in the back of my ambulance *again*!" That's not in the textbook, either.

During this same period, I had also joined the fire department in Sheakleyville, Pennsylvania and had been a member for quite a few years. Additionally, I had joined the Greenville Volunteer Fire Department as a minuteman. By now, you've probably figured out that my world revolved around EMS and fire service. One night, we were dispatched for a motor vehicle accident just south of Greenville. When we arrived on scene, we found a heavily damaged car with a hole through the windshield. But the driver was not to be found.

Police finally tracked him down approximately four blocks away from where the accident occurred. We found him drunker than a skunk with a huge bash on his forehead from where his head had gone through the windshield. He had tried to flee the scene, and now that he was caught, was belligerent, cussing—everything but pleasant.

My partner Kevin and I were amused at the short little cop who took this guy and read him his Miranda rights. The cop gave him a choice: "You can either ride in the back of the ambulance to the hospital or you can go in the cruiser." I was silently praying, "Please go in the cruiser," because I didn't want this idiot puking all over the back of my ambulance. Much to my dismay, but not surprise, he decided I might be more lenient with him in the back of my ambulance than the cops would be if he were riding in the cruiser. Reluctantly, we loaded him on the gurney and we began our transport to the Greenville hospital.

When we got to West Main Street, I knew it was coming. He had to throw up. And of course, I was in the back. I hate the smell of beer puke. Not only was he throwing up, but he was cussing at me and being even more belligerent than he'd been on the scene.

I hollered up to my partner, who was driving, "Kevin, let's go!" All I could hear were the low tones of Kevin's laughter from the front of the ambulance: "Heh, heh, heh, heh, heh." I wasn't sure whose chops I wanted to bust more, my partner's or the drunk's.

One night while I was off duty, the Sheakleyville Fire Department was called around 1:00 a.m. to respond to a motorcycle accident not far from my home. Four motorcycles traveling together had been riding hard all night. Just for fun, some of them wanted to see what speeds they could attain from the skating rink to the curve a few hundred feet away. This was less than a quarter of a mile from where we lived.

One of the riders peeled out and gunned it. Unfortunately, he hit a stone or some debris, which kicked his bike to the left and caused his foot peg to catch the pavement, which then forced him back over to the right side and into a slide. He was still connected to the bike and at some point when the bike swung around, his head with helmet came in full contact with a four-by-four-inch-thick mailbox post. Still connected to the bike, he slid several more yards through a limestone-lined culvert alongside the road. The state police calculated that he had been traveling somewhere around 95 to 100 mph.

In all of my career, I had never seen a helmet or a person's head damaged so badly. The side of the helmet was split in two and had been jerked off his head. My partner Matt and I had the unfortunate job of picking him up and putting him in the body bag. I took hold of his head as we tried to load him in the bag. It felt like a busted coconut. There was brain matter and brain tissue splattered down along the culvert.

Shortly after, I found myself out along the backside of the rescue truck just wanting to heave my guts out. What I had just witnessed made me nauseated.

It's hard to go back to bed after a call like that. Here I am lying beside my wife feeling like I want to puke. I tried to explain it to her, but she couldn't understand. There was no way to make her understand what I had just been through.

Another one that I'll never forget happened when I was off duty at home, but was on call if needed as a backup unit. We got a call for a shooting that occurred in a little town just a few miles from my home, and I was activated for the second ambulance.

There had been a love feud, and the estranged husband was upset because his wife was with another man. The estranged husband had been driving back and forth in front of his ex-wife's and her boyfriend's home. The boyfriend went out to confront him: "Hey, man, you gotta quit this." This happened several times throughout the afternoon and evening.

Around about 7:00, the estranged husband took out a 9 mm pistol and shot the boyfriend in the back nine times. He was already dead when the first unit arrived. Then the shooter turned the 9 mm on himself and shot himself in the head. The entrance wound was a tiny hole in front of the left ear. But the exit wound was a massive hole on the other side, just above his right ear. He was mortally wounded but still breathing, and although we knew he wouldn't make it, we were compelled by law to do what we could.

I'll never forget my feelings while working on that guy. I knew that he had done the shooting and had just killed a man. In my heart I was thinking, "This man deserves to die." But we continued running the code—advanced life support procedures—on him all the way to the hospital.

Seeing these things messes with your head and will often drive you to do things you normally wouldn't do and cause you to think things you normally wouldn't think. In situations like this, my wife was not there to share my pain. She wouldn't have been able to understand.

Take the day we were called to respond to South Second Street in Greenville, to the home of a man who had been missing for two weeks. After the police broke through the door, we were greeted by a swarm of flies and a stench that brought tears to my eyes. The man had been dead, lying in ninety-five-degree weather for almost two weeks, and my partner Matt and I were left to clean up the mess.

The only people who could understand our reactions to these situations were our partners, the people with whom we worked side-by-side. Men and women, we lived in the same quarters for twenty-four hours at a time, ate our meals together, and slept side by side on the bunks. We responded together to every sort of situation imaginable.

After a while, you bonded. You became very close to the people you worked with, and in many ways you became closer to them than to your immediate family. Oftentimes, we talked each other down, cried together, and dealt with it together. These were the men and women who served with you in the trenches every day. This closeness with my partners was very instrumental in and had much to do with some of the problems that Trish and I were experiencing.

I have great respect for the men and women who work in the EMS world. However, looking back, I would have handled things much differently had I been a Christian, fully devoted to Christ. My demeanor, my language and my actions and reactions would have been different. It is very tough to maintain any level of Christianity working in this profession because of great temptations, but it can be done. Philippians 4:13 says, "I can do all things through Christ which strengtheneth me."

By the time it was all over, I'd spent seventeen years of my life in EMS, pre-hospital care and fire service. We dealt with traumatic situations every day, a whole different world from the one I shared with Trish. The EMS world was filled with gunshots, stabbings, hangings and mangled bodies trapped inside wrecked cars. The stresses, the circumstances and the inability to share that world helped propel my free-fall into drinking, cheating on my wife, and the day that I would walk out on my family.

CHAPTER 8

Close Calls

Our voices have resounded on radio stations across the country, singing songs of praise and adoration to the King of Kings. It's only by the grace of God that my name wasn't heard instead on the evening news in the tale of another tragic fatality. I've had many close encounters with death over the years.

One particular night on my way home from a date with Trish in Hadley, I fell asleep at the wheel of my old Plymouth. At this time, I had only a junior driver's license and was required to be home by midnight. It had been a long weekend, and I was very tired. The last thing I remember was crossing the causeway on Route 422 at Moraine State Park, about 30 miles from my home in Worthington. Just after crossing the bridge, I fell asleep. God only knows how I managed to make it around the next turn while asleep at the wheel.

What I remember next was the sound of metal against metal. I was thrown from the driver's seat to the passenger's side of the car, my head bouncing off the inside doorframe. I had hit the guardrails on the right side of the road, which threw me into a spin. In my panic, I instinctively reached for the steering wheel. I grabbed at the wheel, it jerked, and the car shot to the left across my two lanes of traffic, proceeded down through the median and across the two oncoming lanes of traffic. Somehow, miraculously, it ended up right side up on all four wheels on the far embankment.

When the dust settled, I looked down a very steep hill, probably a good 25 feet off the road. I didn't make it home before midnight. Now all I had to do was figure out a way to get the car off the hillside. Thanks to my

Uncle Don and Dad, the old Plymouth was retrieved, and after repairing the bent frame and a right fender, the old girl was back on the road.

Then there was the Sunday morning when Trish and I were traveling on very bad roads on our way to Rimersburg. We were on our way to church, and just outside the little town of Sligo, Pennsylvania, I lost control of the car. We hit a brand new Crown Victoria and literally destroyed the entire side of that car. Once again, I was driving the old Plymouth Fury . . . that car was like a cat with nine lives! We just kept putting it back on the road after each accident.

And in every instance, God was reminding me that He cared for me and was constantly watching over me. He was saying, "If it wasn't for Me, you wouldn't be here."

Mom and Dad used to laugh when I was a volunteer firefighter in Worthington because I could be lying in a deep sleep but still hear the click of the siren before it started to wail. When the siren started, it made a clicking noise. I'd hear that click and pop up and run out the door.

One Sunday afternoon while Trish and I were dating, I was lying on the couch with my head in her lap, and you guessed it, I heard *the click*. I was up and running. I nearly scared her to death. She sputtered, "Wha... wha... whatta you doin'?" until she heard the siren start a few seconds later. Then she knew.

After marrying Trish and moving to Hadley, I became a member of the Sheakleyville Community Volunteer Fire Department. It was my nature, tired or not, to respond to every call. It was in my blood.

Let me take you to Halloween Day 1988, just an absolutely crazy day. I had come off a twenty-four-hour shift on the ambulance and was extremely tired. Trish and I were living in a trailer park on Grandview Drive in Hadley. Shortly after I dragged home from work, my pager went off. The fire department was dispatched to a rescue call down on the old Conrail tracks, not far from where we lived.

When we arrived on scene, we found our patient. He had an open compound fracture of the tibia-fibula on his right leg. He had been working on a flatbed truck and a piece of iron rail they were loading swung around and caught him on the leg, knocking him down into the ditch along the tracks. The ambulance was not able to get back to where we were, so we simply stabilized him and transported him out in the bed of a pickup truck to the main road.

After we were cleared from the call, I walked back into the house and started to relax when the pager went off again. This time, it was a structure fire just four doors down from where we lived. I always carried my gear with me, and I was first on the scene.

The kitchen and the whole front end of the house were fully involved. I didn't know if there was anyone inside. The neighbors didn't know either but thought there may have been a dog in the house. I busted through the front door and yelled for anybody to answer, but the intense heat and smoke turned me away. I didn't have an air pack, and no fire engines were on scene yet.

When the engines arrived, we knocked down the fire and contained it to just the front of the house. During our search and rescue procedures, thankfully, we found no humans, but we did find the dog. He didn't survive.

During cleanup, our department was dispatched on yet another call. This call was for a structure fire on Yeager Road. An Amish home was on fire. Our fire chief, Bill, hollered at me and our fire captain, "Jake, I want you to take Randy and go directly to the scene. Mutual aid departments are responding and we will meet you there as soon as we are finished mopping up."

When we got there, fire was already shooting through the roof. The structure was fully involved. It was really cooking! I knew in my heart that the home would be a total loss. It was another one of those times to "surround and drown."

Jake hollered, "Randy, when the trucks get here, get on a hose line." We knew there would be no way to make an interior attack. It would be exterior operations only. About a week earlier, I had received new turnout gear from the department and was just getting it broken in. When the trucks finally arrived, I was geared up and ready to go.

A truck from Sandy Lake, Pennsylvania, Volunteer Fire Department was first on the scene, and I immediately did as instructed and grabbed a one-and-a-half-inch hose line. I had two other firefighters from Sandy Lake backing me up. My crew worked the left side of the house facing the road. When the line was charged, I adjusted the nozzle stream so the water arced down through the roof.

The next thing I remember was Jake screaming, *"Randy! Look out!"* From the corner of my left eye, I caught a glimpse of a huge, black mass, hurtling toward me. Instinctively, I shut down the hose line while taking a step to the right in an attempt to run. It was already too late. I made it about a half a step and was flattened like a pancake.

Ray, an EMT with Sandy Lake Ambulance and an old Army medic, told me later, "Randy, you hit the ground so hard that you bounced. You came down and it was like the recoil brought you back up off the ground."

What had happened was that somebody on a hose line on the right side of the house hit the chimney with his stream of water. Due to the intense heat, the chimney was unstable and detached from the house. The huge black mass that I saw out of the corner of my eye was the chimney falling. The highest clump of bricks that hit me caught me at the base of the neck. Had it been a little bit higher, it would have killed me. The thoracic and lumbar regions of my back bore the brunt of the impact.

As I was hurled to the ground, my life flashed before me. I saw my kids, Trish, everything. It was surreal. I thought I was a goner. Through it all, I never lost consciousness but was in terrific pain and could not feel anything on my left side from my hip all the way down to the bottom of my foot. It was numb. It was almost as if I had been paralyzed on my left side.

Immediately, fellow EMS personnel and firefighters were at my side. My brand new turnout gear that I was breaking in was cut off of me. But that was the least of my concerns—in the process, they also cut off my pants.

Here I was, the paramedic who was always working on somebody else, and now I was the patient. The roles had been reversed. I was quickly immobilized and minutes later found myself in the back of Sandy Lake's ambulance as they rushed me to the hospital. En route, they called for a paramedic assist from the company I actually worked for, Gold Cross Ambulance. It was none other than my friends and colleagues George and Jerry who responded.

Coincidentally, they met us right at the end of the driveway of our home. George had just a few seconds to run to the house and knock on the door. When Trish answered, George said, "I just wanted to let you know that Randy's on the ambulance." This was not an uncommon thing for Trish to hear. I would often accompany the ambulance to the hospital on medical calls.

Things became very clear to her when George put his arm around her shoulder and said, "No, dear, Randy's the patient."

On the way to the hospital, Autumn, an EMT with Sandy Lake, sat behind me on the jump seat and put an oxygen mask on my face. I was fully immobilized, unable to move and extremely nauseated. I was so sick. I remember saying, "I'm going to throw up. I'm going to throw up." They turned the backboard I was lying on to the side to allow me the opportunity to heave.

Being immobilized, I felt as though I would suffocate. Autumn finally consented to loosen my arms. She said, "Do you need more oxygen?" I said, "Yeah," and I reached up with a loosened arm and adjusted my own oxygen flow.

She said, "Oh, man, you're a terrible patient."

I said, "Turn it up a little bit more."

Although things were very serious, we were laughing. "You're the only guy we know who would adjust his own oxygen on the way to the hospital," she said.

By the time we got there, feeling was beginning to come back into my left leg. Long story short, the X-rays were read and nothing was broken. It was just severe bruising. Basically, my body had borne the brunt of the impact of an entire brick chimney, and I had survived. Another miracle.

At first, the rescue team thought I was in critical condition and would probably never walk again. However, with the aid of crutches and two weeks of recuperation, I was back on my feet, working again, and going strong.

Now at the age of forty-eight, every time a change occurs in the weather, I am reminded of that incident, as I still experience pain in my lower back and left leg—a reminder of God's hand of protection on my life.

CHAPTER 9

Despicable Me

My life was EMS and the fire service. I would work twenty-four hours on and forty-eight hours off at the ambulance station. If somebody couldn't come in, I might find myself working another twelve-hour shift. There were many times that I ended up working thirty-six hours straight. During the tornadoes of 1985—one roaring just north of Greenville that nearly wiped out the little town of Atlantic, and another sweeping to the south of Greenville through Hermitage and Wheatland in the Shenango Valley—I worked nearly forty-eight hours straight.

On the afternoon of the tornadoes, the air was thick with humidity and a yellow haze hung in the atmosphere. I was off duty that day. Trish and I were living with her parents at the time with our son Jeffrey. In the late afternoon/early evening, we needed to make a trip to Meadville, Pennsylvania, and while traveling on Route 19 North, we saw something big and black move across the road in front of us. We saw debris, especially a piece of green awning floating in the air, but we did not see a funnel cloud. Whatever it was, it ripped across the road in front of us about 30 seconds before we arrived near the intersection of Route 19 and Adamsville Road.

When we arrived at the intersection, we knew exactly what had happened. Trees were down, houses were damaged and we knew that a tornado just roared through.

It didn't take long until I was activated and was asked to dispatch our units from Greenville because the radio antenna and phone lines were down and everything was being directed over to our station. Additionally, the hospital morgue was full and a temporary morgue was set up in our station garage. That night, we had five bodies there as a result of the devastation.

Needless to say, I spent all that night at the station answering phones and dispatching units, then worked a complete twenty-four-hour shift the next day and an additional twelve-hour shift the following day.

Throughout my EMS career, there were many situations like that one which required multiple hours of service. Maintaining a schedule like this is not good for the home life. On top of all this, there was the fire service, paramedic classes two nights a week, required clinical time in the hospital to maintain my IV and drug therapy skills and EKG interpretation. And if that wasn't enough, at different times throughout my career I often coordinated and instructed EMT classes run by the Pennsylvania Department of Health at Sharon Regional Hospital.

I was never home.

I was always working—often with members of the opposite sex. At work, we basically lived in paramilitary conditions, always in uniform, with our own quarters, complete with lounge, bunk room and kitchen. On duty, we slept, ate, and entertained ourselves between calls. We played a lot of basketball and ping pong on slow days. In the evenings, we watched TV together until it was time to hit the bunk. We were like family. We had our own little lifestyle. And we were always on edge, waiting for the next call.

After work, it was time to go home. Oh yeah, that's where my wife and my kids lived, the other family I had. At the time, I felt as though I lived in two different worlds. Not to use this as a crutch, but during the countless hours spent away from home, I, just like so many of my friends, was out there facing the trauma and the blood and guts. Quite honestly, at twenty-one or twenty-two years old, I was not mature enough to deal with the things I was seeing.

I loved Trish, I really did. But she couldn't understand what I was going through. She couldn't see the pain on tortured faces, smell the hot oil spilling out of a mangled car, or feel the warmth of fresh blood against surgical gloves while desperately trying to stop the bleeding. It seemed like Trish and I were worlds apart.

One day while running a call at a local nursing home, a good-looking lady who worked there caught my attention. All it took was a look. I obviously caught her attention as well. I heard her say, "Hey good looking, how're you doing?" That was it. I was hooked. The dragon had been unleashed.

It was like a fire that could not be quenched. I was on a downward spiral that would lead me not only into her arms, but into multiple affairs and a lifestyle that I would deeply regret. The songwriter was correct when he said sin will take you farther and cost you far more than you ever thought you would go or have to pay.

The more I became involved in the world of EMS, the more my life became a quagmire of entanglement which acted as a great cover and excuse for my sin. It wasn't a matter of *if* I would be with another woman, it was a matter of *when*. It consumed my every waking moment.

Sir Walter Scott wrote, *"Oh what a tangled web we weave / When first we practice to deceive."* Just like the black widow spinning a web to catch her prey, Satan had spun his web very well, and every day I was entangling myself deeper and deeper.

I never had really gotten to know Trish like I should have. It wasn't her fault. I never gave her a chance, nor did I take the time. I was always too busy doing my own thing and following after my own pursuits.

Likewise, I didn't have time to spend with my kids or get to know them like a good father should. I regret that to this day. When I was at home, I seriously tried in my crippled way to spend time with the kids, and we did have a few good times. But my mind was always distracted as I was scheming and planning for the next time when I would be able to give in to my own reckless pursuits and self-gratification.

I lived a double life for so long that I mastered every excuse in the book for why I would be late or not coming home at all. I invented reasons. I had the prime opportunity because I was working EMS, and she was used to my not being there and always gave me the benefit of the doubt. She wanted to believe in her husband. But I was away from her so much that I could basically come and go as I pleased with zero accountability.

Call it a moment of weakness or divine providence, but one night I finally had the nerve to confess everything to Trish. I had to tell her about the double life I had been living. One night while on our way home from Hermitage, we pulled over to the side of the road not far from the place where the seventeen-year-old girl was killed near Wasser Bridge Road and

Route 18, and I poured my heart out to Trish. When we were dating, she was always quick to lend a listening ear, and that night I just felt like I needed someone to whom I could confess the lies and convoluted life I was living. By this time, I didn't care anymore. The consequences didn't matter. I was in over my head, and I was numb.

Trish was a gem. By the world's standards, she would have had every right to walk out the door and never look back. But she didn't. This was one of the qualities I hated at the time. When she refused to let me go, this made me angrier and more frustrated. I wanted her to let me go and was hoping she would agree to a divorce. But she wouldn't. She just wouldn't let go.

Although I had confessed my infidelity to her, that did not deter my promiscuous lifestyle. Even though some of her family said, "Let him go. He's crazy. He's out of his mind," she said, "No," reminding them that from the first time she ever told me she loved me, she knew it was for real.

At the times when I did come home, she would iron my shirts, wash my clothes, and prepare meals if needed. She did anything she could to make me comfortable. And I just walked right over top of her, never giving a thought to her comfort.

I'll never forget the night—it still haunts me—that I was going to Pittsburgh for a concert and planned to spend the night with someone else. Trish actually ironed my white shirt before I left. Although she didn't know the details, her perception was keen. She asked me, "You're going with ---- tonight?" and called her by name. And I said, "Yeah."

It was killing her, and I understand now it was ripping her heart out. In previous conversations with Trish, I had told her I did not understand what love was all about, and somehow through her pain, she was showing me what God's love was like—it's unconditional. Although I didn't appreciate it at the time, as I look back, if there was any person who came close to walking on water, it was my wife.

I was so frustrated. I hated God. I hated my job. I hated everything there was to hate about my life. I finally thought, "Well if she's not going to throw me out, I'm just going to leave on my own." One Sunday evening after a short visit at home, I broke the news to her, "Trish, I don't love you anymore, and I'm leaving."

Crying uncontrollably, she begged me to stay. Embracing me, she pleaded with me not to go. "Honey, why do you have to go?" she asked.

"Trish, I just have to go. You're going to have to let me go."

I remember walking into the bathroom, putting the toilet lid down and sitting on the edge of the toilet. I pulled my two boys, Jeff and Doug, close to me. Tears streamed down their faces as I told them, "Boys, Dad's leaving. I'm going to leave."

The boys pleaded with me. "Daddy, why do you gotta go? Why do you gotta go?" I said, "I don't know boys. I gotta go. I just gotta go. I can't live like this anymore."

At this time, Lynn was so young that she didn't comprehend what was going on.

For the next fifteen to eighteen months, I was gone. Trish never knew if I was coming or going. I stayed mostly in the house where my office was. By this time, I was director of marketing and public relations for Gold Cross Ambulance in Mercer County. I had a couch. I had a bathroom. I could take showers right next door at the ambulance station. I had everything I needed—or so I thought. I even did a little bit of my own laundry, but not too much. Trish pretty much kept that stuff up for me even after all I had done to hurt her. She was amazing.

By now, I used alcohol freely. It all started at a Christmas party at work with an open bar. I had my first drink, which led to many more. I was twenty-five years old, and never before had I ever had a drop of alcohol.

One night, two of the guys from work took me out to Fyetta's Athletic Club, a bar in Greenville that is no longer open. I don't know why, but this night stands out clearly in my mind ahead of so many other nights. My friends said, "Whatever we buy, you drink tonight." And I said, "Yeah, man, bring it on. I'll do whatever."

We were doing shots of Ouzo and Blue Hawaiian. Ouzo is a licorice-tasting hard liquor, probably about 80 proof, nasty stuff, and we were doing shots of it. One of the cardinal rules of drinking is that you should stay on the same drink all evening. Not this night. In addition to ouzo and Blue Hawaiian, we were drinking mixed drinks—rum and Coke, fuzzy navels (a peach-flavored drink) and wine coolers. It didn't matter. I was drinking anything I could get my hands on. Anything they bought was going down the hatch.

The boys told me, "You're going to be sick in the morning."

About halfway through the evening, I had to go to the bathroom. That's when it hit me like a ton of bricks. The room spun. Man, I tried to reach the floor with my foot, and it felt like I was stepping off into the abyss. Somehow I managed to make it to the bathroom and back to the bar, where we continued our drinking.

When my buddies dropped me off that night, I remember one of them saying, "You're gonna be sick in the morning." About a half hour later, I woke up and for some reason had the urge to go home. I got in my truck and I drove the eight miles to Hadley. I can't remember any of the drive other than passing the Country Fair gas station on the outskirts of Greenville and pulling into the driveway at the trailer park. Everything else in between is a blur. I shouldn't even be alive today to tell about this incident.

When I walked through the door, Trish said, "You've been drinking."

And I said, "Yeah." I laid down on the couch in the living room where I slept all night. I got up the next morning without a trace of a headache or nausea, and went back to work. That's a God thing. That's the only way I can explain it.

It was like being sucked into quicksand. The more I hated my life and everything about it, the deeper into the pit I went. I was frustrated, with a deep sense of loneliness. I needed change. And the only option I could see was suicide.

My life was a living hell, and I had turned my back on anyone and everyone who ever cared about me. I thought, "I'm so sick of living this life. I'm going to end it all. This is it. I'm done." Many times before, I'd taunted my wife with a little bullet that I carried with me in my pocket. "This is my ticket. Someday, I'm going to use it." I knew this was breaking her heart, as she was on an emotional roller coaster, wanting so badly for me to straighten out.

In Pennsylvania, the bars used to close on Sundays. So one Sunday night, I drove out over West Main Hill toward Ohio to the little town of Vienna, about 25 miles away from Greenville, where I knew there was a Dairy Mart where I could buy alcohol on Sunday. In addition to the black cherry wine coolers, I bought a carton of salty crackers.

Ironically, Vienna, Ohio, is the same town where Northeast Ohio Bible Institute is located, the school I would attend years later in preparation for ordination.

That night, I said to myself, "I'm going to get enough alcohol in me to make myself numb because tonight is the night I'm going to end it all."

The minute I left Vienna, I started drinking. I drank the whole way back to Greenville. By the time I got back to my office, the entire carton was gone. When I walked in the door, I thought, "In the morning, they're going to have a bloody mess to clean up."

I kept a gun underneath the couch. I sat on the edge of the couch, took out the pistol, a .380 semi-automatic, loaded it, pulled the hammer back and put the gun up to the side of my head.

This was it.

This was another moment when my life seemed to stand still. I was one trigger pull away from death, and yet God was continuing to be faithful to me. As I sat there, thoughts flooded my mind. It was as if God was speaking to me. "Randy, you know if you pull this trigger, you're going to go to hell. And the hell you're going to go to is far worse than the hell you think you're living in now."

Immediately, I heard flashbacks of sermons from my childhood years, flashbacks of evangelists talking about people committing suicide. I remembered them saying, "If you commit suicide, if you take your own life, you're going to die and go straight to hell."

In that moment, time seemed to stand still. My whole life flashed before me again, scenes from childhood, school days, early married life and kids. Everything came rushing back to me like videotape on overdrive.

For no other explanation than God, sanity took over, and I uncocked the hammer of the gun, unloaded it and put it back underneath the couch. Seconds later, I lay down and drifted off into a deep sleep.

I realized that night in some crazy way that God loved me and cared about me. God's love is amazing. It's unconditional. He loves us no matter where we've been or what we've done. It doesn't matter how evil, mean or rotten that we've been, or how badly we have hurt the people who love us the most. He's always there with arms open wide, ready to welcome us home.

CHAPTER 10

A Sweet-Smelling Savor

During the time I was estranged from the family, I allowed my animal instincts to guide me. I am greatly ashamed about the level of depravation into which I sunk. Misuse of alcohol and running like a dog, coupled with my frustration and depression—my life remained a living hell.

Through it all, Trish maintained her composure and remained firm in her convictions and love for me. I couldn't understand it. I wanted her to hate me. And yet *she refused to let go.*

On occasions when I had to be back at the house with Trish and the kids, she would always tell me that she loved me and was praying for me. This utterly frustrated me. I didn't want her to care. I didn't want her to love me. I wanted her to let me go, so the guilt and pressure I felt for not facing my responsibilities like a real man would be eased.

Trish was on a mission. Through her actions, she was showing me what unconditional love was all about. And I hated it!

Every time she said, "Randy, I love you, and I'm praying for you," I wanted to grab her and choke the life out of her because it made me insanely frustrated. I didn't want her to love me. I wanted her to hate me, to throw me aside. I already felt evil and dirty. I just wanted her to give up on me, leave me alone, and quit trying.

I remember saying to her, "I want you to hate me. *I'm not worth being loved.*" But again she would say it: "I love you, and I'm praying for you."

Oh, *this woman*, she was driving me crazy. She was relentless in her pursuit.

Then came the day—the only time she didn't say it.

It was deer season, and I decided to go hunting. I was never a great hunter, but I occasionally enjoyed going out into the woods. I stopped at the house to pick up my deer rifle and some hunting supplies. I planned to hunt down over the hill from where Trish and the kids lived along the Little Shenango River. I gathered up my equipment and walked out of the trailer, knowing that I would hear those dreaded words again.

To my amazement, she remained silent.

I stood at the end of the sidewalk. You could have knocked me over with a feather. This was strange. She didn't say it. I guess way down deep in the depths of my soul, I really wanted to know that someone cared.

I turned back, and I looked at Trish. "Well? Aren't you going to say it?" She said, "I didn't think you wanted me to say it anymore."

The next words out of my mouth surprised me: "Don't give up on me."

Maybe it was a moment of weakness. I don't know. Whatever the case, it was another one of those God things. I really didn't want her to give up on me.

Again, some of her family encouraged Trish to let me go. They said, "He's crazy. He's out of his mind." Trish held her ground, reminding them, "From the first time I ever told that boy that I loved him, I knew it was for real."

And once again that morning, she said the words that I thought I didn't want to hear: "Randy, I love you and I'm praying for you."

Until the day I die, I will never forget February of 1993. I was sleeping on the couch in the office where I worked. Between 3 and 4 a.m., I was awakened from a sound sleep. It seemed as though Trish's presence hovered near me or looked down on me as I slept. It was so real that it woke me up.

The phone was on the floor beside me. It was one of those old phones with the large push buttons, so I could dial numbers in the dark. I picked up the phone and punched in Trish's number. When she answered, I said, "Trish, were you just here in my office?" She said, "No."

"Are you sure you weren't here?" She said, "Why are you calling me at this hour of the morning to ask me this? Are you crazy?" I said, "I woke up and it just seemed like you were here."

She was silent.

Then I asked, "What were you doing?"

And she said, "Why are you asking?"

That's when the light turned on. "Were you praying for me?"

"Yes."

Let me tell you something. That morning, for the first time, I started to have a profound awareness for what love was all about. Trish was a desperate woman willing to give up or do anything to see her husband's life turned around.

In her mind, Trish had built an imaginary altar. She placed herself and the kids on that imaginary altar and said, "God, whatever it takes to see Randy get saved, I'm willing to go through it, even if it means I have to lose my life or the life of one of our kids to get his attention."

I found out later that Trish had been fasting and praying for me for nearly two weeks. She lost weight, dropping to 86 pounds, and she wasn't a big woman to begin with. She told me later that during this time of fasting that she had had maybe three solid hours of sleep and maybe two full meals. In addition to taking care of the kids and maintaining the house, she read her Bible and songs out of the hymnal to keep her awake while she spent her nights praying for my transformation.

During this time, God gave her a promise from Isaiah 55:11, where it says, "So shall my word be that goeth forth out of my mouth: It shall not return unto me void, but it shall accomplish that which I please, and it shall prosper in the thing whereto I sent it." She claimed that promise and held onto it. She said, "God, Your promises are true, and one of these days—I don't know when, but in Your time—I'm going to see Randy turn his attention toward You and get saved."

Just a few weeks earlier I had considered moving in with another woman, but to my surprise, the other woman refused. She said, "You're not ready, because you haven't let go of your wife and your kids." If she had consented, undoubtedly I would have ended up divorced and my story would be totally different today. To my amazement, God actually used her to get my thinking process back on track.

I truly believe that when I was awakened early that morning in February, it was the first step of Trish's promise being fulfilled. It was the turning point, the high-water mark in my unsaved life. I knew down deep in my heart that change was in the wind. That morning I realized, "Here

I am running, doing everything I can to suppress and put down the only person who truly loves me other than God Himself."

She would have died for me in an instant, and I finally understood it. With her, the past didn't matter, and she was willing to forgive. She just wanted me home with her and the kids.

Thankfully, I made the decision to move back home with the family. I would like to say everything changed immediately, but a baby doesn't learn to walk in one day. And I had just taken my first baby step toward change.

Even though I was at home, my personal life remained a mess, and I continued my illicit lifestyle. I still wasn't saved. I still hadn't surrendered my will to God.

But my wife had prayed me home. It was a start.

CHAPTER 11

Murderous Intent

A few weeks after I moved back home, my barber called and wanted me to see a new business venture that he and his wife had just gotten into. Due to my work schedule, I kept declining the offers of his repeated calls. Finally, he said, "Randy, you've just got to see this. You're an outgoing person. You like people. This will be a great business opportunity for you."

So after much persistence on his part, we consented to travel to his home in Worthington to see this new thing. When we arrived at the appointed time, a few other people were there. We watched a video, and then to my surprise, the photographer from our wedding stood up to speak. He was in the business.

He began drawing circles on a dry erase board. After drawing the first circle, he said, "This is you." He drew six legs coming off the circle, put one circle at the bottom of each leg and said, "Now think of the names of your relatives, neighbors, friends, and colleagues whom you can place in each of the other six circles."

If you haven't figured it out yet, we were being introduced for the very first time to a multi-level network marketing business, Amway.

During the meeting, they asked us what our dreams were. Trish said she'd like to have a Lincoln Town Car. That dream never came true. I couldn't have cared less. I just wanted the money. That dream never came true, either.

Well, we saw the plan, we bought the plan, and we started selling the plan. They told us that we were diamonds in the rough, just needing to be refined. They also said that if we showed the plan at least twenty times a month, we would be well on our way to having a successful business.

This was going to be easy. I knew I could draw circles.

Call it a good thing or a bad thing, I'm not sure which, but it's my nature that whatever I'm involved in, I'm in all the way, totally committed. Even to this day, if I see an open door or an opportunity, I usually drive right through it without reading directions or giving it proper research. Maybe it's a guy thing. Hopefully, after some years of experience, I'll start to get it right.

This was the first thing that Trish and I were ever committed to. In fact, it was the first thing that we ever worked at together, which was a good thing.

During the first few months, I was gung-ho, head over heels. I would have shown the plan to a monkey if he'd listen. They said that we should show the plan to our relatives and everybody we came in contact with, and we did.

One night while showing the plan to my parents, my dad made a statement that sent me into a frenzy. What he said unleashed the beast that lurked inside of me, nearly resulting in a very deadly outcome. However, once again, God was there to intervene, and He used Trish as His tool.

Although it was correct, the statement Dad made couldn't have come at a worse time. He reminded me that my number one priority was to take care of my own responsibilities and my family. Please understand that after years of neglecting my responsibilities, I felt as though I *was* finally facing life and stepping up to the plate to take care of my family. I was on edge, and his statements pushed me to the other side.

I exploded.

All the anger, frustration and venom pent up for years, all the memories of his merciless beatings and abuse burst. Just like Mount St. Helens, I exploded, spewing hot streams of lava everywhere. There were things said and done that night that I wish had never happened and my children hadn't had to witness.

There was so much hatred and rage coming out of me. I invented words. Anything I could think of, I called him. It flowed out of me. All the pain, everything that my life had become was now *his* fault! Or so I thought. I was really good at pointing the blame at others for my failures, but not so good at seeing that the cause of my trouble was coming from the face looking back at me in the mirror.

I decided to end this miserable man's life.

Trish, who is only five feet tall and weighed about ninety-three pounds at the time, was doing everything she could do to hold me back. She had superhuman strength that night.

The scuffle continued for a period of time until finally I was completely over the edge. Something had snapped in my mind. I looked at my father and said, "You are a dead man. I am going to kill you. I would rather sit in jail the rest of my life than to see you take another breath."

Trish could tell by the look in my eye that somehow I had crossed the threshold and was no longer in control. She told me later, "I will never forget the look in your eyes. It was like something glazed them over and you descended to another realm, not of this world."

In that terrible moment, you can only imagine what my children were thinking. I'm sorry they had to see me in this condition, and I regret it to this day. No child should ever see his or her father behave in such a manner. In situations like these, it's always the kids who get hurt and suffer the most. It leaves lasting impressions and often brings unnecessary baggage that they will carry with them for the rest of their lives.

I had a .380 semi-automatic pistol in the truck, and Trish knew exactly what was going to happen. Call it a miracle, call it unbelievable, call it whatever you want, but somehow amid all the pushing and shoving, my two boys screaming and crying, "Daddy, Daddy," and the whole insanity of the moment, Trish was able to slip past and make it out the door in front of me, thus beating me to the truck. When she got there, she grabbed the pistol from underneath the seat and took off running down Virgin Alley as fast as she could toward Main Street in Worthington.

By now I was so far out of control that had I been able to get my hands on the gun, there's no doubt in my mind that there would have been seven bodies for the police to deal with. My anger had turned from my dad and was now against my wife, and had I been able to get ahold of her, I would have killed her. I craved killing my father, but she stood in my way, and I would have been willing to do anything to clear the path. I wanted the pain and the insanity to end.

After a few moments in the cold, night air, my feelings and my senses started to come back, after which my thinking faculties started to return.

Mom took Dad into another room, and I was allowed back into their house to retrieve our belongings. The last words I remember saying to my dad on the way out the door were, "You are not my father. My father is dead. And if you ever step foot on my property, I will take the shotgun, and I will blow your head off your shoulders."

Trish and I gathered up the kids and headed back to Hadley. I wept—tears of remorse, regret, hopelessness. It was the longest seventy-mile trip I'd ever been on.

About two weeks later, my dad called to apologize in his crippled way, but I had vowed that I would never speak to him or have anything to do with him again. Reluctantly, I agreed to accept his apology, but I was still really cold toward him. How could a man who professed to be saved and sanctified act in such a manner? This was all confusing to me.

Later in June, Trish and I attended a huge business seminar in King of Prussia, near Philadelphia. There were probably 10,000 to 15,000 people in the convention center. It was amazing. The core beliefs of the Amway Corporation were God, family, and country, and they practiced what they preached. I'll never regret our time spent in the business as I learned much about myself.

On the Sunday morning of the business seminar, they had a worship service, complete with a brass ensemble that played "Amazing Grace." Ironically, the Baptist minister who preached delivered a powerful message on how husbands ought to take care of their responsibilities at home: namely, their wives and their children. While he preached, I wanted to crawl under the table. Trish thought I might go forward when the altar call was given, but I still wasn't ready.

That was in June of 1993. My time would come on August 18th of 1993. That was the night I got saved and accepted Christ as my Savior. When I got up from the altar that night, the first person I saw was my dad kneeling beside me. He was weeping too. We embraced, and he said, "Son, I saw you go forward tonight, and you put me under conviction."

Let me tell you about that night.

CHAPTER 12

Forgiven

August 18, 1993—that was the day I came back to the land of the living, spiritually speaking.

I told you in the first chapter how the evangelist preached a message about the straight and narrow way. One of the things that made a lasting impression on my mind that night happened while he was preaching, and several people in the congregation stood, shouting praises to God and waving their arms. A few of the ladies waved their handkerchiefs in the air. It was amazing. They were free. People were on their feet all over the tabernacle praising God.

Meanwhile, I was sitting there in the same tabernacle, the same church camp, not far from the very place where a few years earlier I laid eyes for the first time on the girl who would become my wife. Conflict raged in my mind. The Holy Spirit confronted me with the life I had been living and the hopelessness of my situation unless I repented. With my thoughts whirling, I suddenly realized that what I really needed was what these folks were shouting about. They had peace; they had assurance; and they knew where they were going if they died.

They had what I so desperately desired.

When the altar call was given, I found myself standing with tears streaming down my face, gripping the back of the pew in front of me. For the first time in my life, God was showing me my life as though it were being projected on a screen.

I had finally reached the breaking point. I couldn't hold out any longer, and just like the Prodigal Son who came to himself and returned to his father, I knew what I had to do. With a little coaxing from a nearby pastor who said, "Randy, why don't you just go up to the altar and get it settled," I stepped into the aisle. Until this point, I had been traveling the long road. But now, finally, I was coming home.

By this time, the entire congregation was on its feet singing a song of invitation. I can't remember what they sang. It doesn't really matter. I was desperate for change, and I was focused on attaining that goal.

I believe in my heart that the work was already done in that I had already surrendered to the Master when I stepped into the aisle. But I still needed to go forward to humble myself on the altar, where for about twenty minutes, tears flowed uncontrollably. I simply poured out my entire heart and confessed every sin that I could remember to the Savior.

For the first time in my life, I became really honest with God, admitting that I had been a failure as a person, a failure as a husband, and a failure as a dad. I had made a mess of everything. My life was a wreck. I had turned my back on my wife and my kids and lived the life of a fool.

I said, "God, if You can take all the broken pieces of the puzzle of my life and somehow put them back together again, I will say yes to You for the rest of my life."

As I knelt there, I heard my Uncle Gary praying beside me. Every now and again, I could feel his gigantic hand patting my shoulder as he said, "Tell Him all about it Randy. Tell Jesus all about it."

I loved all of my mother's brothers, but Uncle Gary was special to me because I spent considerable time with him when I was growing up. There were twelve brothers and sisters on Mom's side of the family, the Troup side. All of her brothers had a reputation for being tough, and all were big and over six feet tall. Uncle Gary was the largest of all. He was about six-foot-five and weighed about 400 pounds, a mass of humanity. During high school, Uncle Gary wrestled. He was quite famous in his area and was known as the Marion Center Bear. He was the uncle that everyone bragged on. When we were kids riding the elementary school bus, he was the guy I would threaten the other kids with: "If you don't quit messing with me, I'm going to get my Uncle Gary after you!"

Although he was big, he was a gentle giant. Uncle Gary also had a story to tell of God's amazing grace, and by now, his life had been transformed, and he was a minister of the Gospel. He also had a way about him. When he put his arms around you, you could just feel the love coming from him.

I'll never forget the summer I stayed at his house for two weeks while he was pastor of the Little Hope Church near the town of Northeast, Pennsylvania. Uncle Gary had a knack for finding deals, and it was there that I was introduced to Lunchbox Pies and banana ice cream. He would buy ice cream by the five-quart container, and the servings—man, they were good! And big.

One afternoon I was helping Uncle Gary weed his garden in Little Hope, and a man who was selling insurance walked up and asked if he would like to hear about the insurance he was selling. Uncle Gary responded that he would be willing to listen about the *insurance* if, after the man was finished, Uncle Gary could have the opportunity to tell him about the *assurance*.

We had shared many good memories, but now a new memory that would forever be imprinted on my mind was being made. I heard him encourage me to go all the way to the bottom and pour out all of my frustrations, pain, hurt and anger. He encouraged me just to let go and allow all of my emotions to be exposed into the light of Truth. I was so empty and in desperate need for something to satisfy. Now I was finally experiencing the assurance that Uncle Gary told the insurance man about that day in the garden.

When I finally got up from the altar, I had a peace like I had never known. God had forgiven me! My heart was clean. I could breathe again. I was a brand new man.

A few years later in our ministry, I was talking to an evangelist who was there that night when I got saved. He mentioned that he remembered seeing me praying at the altar but had doubts as to whether I had really gotten saved. He was glad to know that I had gotten the goods. Isn't it amazing how we judge and stereotype people just because of the way they may look or dress?

"Altar nurses" and well-meaning people often will attempt to interfere with the leadings of the Holy Spirit in the life of a new believer. But one of the things that didn't happen that night was that no one approached me with a list of dos and don'ts—things I would have to line up to as a new Christian. I had never been one to be pushed, and when my wife asked me what I was going to do about some of the things I was involved in, my response to her was that I was going to allow the Lord to guide me.

Over the years, I have learned a great lesson. Proverbs 3:5-6 says, "Trust in the Lord with all your heart and lean not unto your own understanding. In all your ways, acknowledge Him and He will direct your paths." I simply needed the Holy Spirit to be my guide. Down deep in my heart, I wanted to please God rather than man, and I was determined to line up with the Bible, not a book of man-made rules.

The devil doesn't miss a trick, and within moments of leaving the altar, I was under demonic attack. Satan was already planting seeds of doubt in my mind. I remember very vividly one of his suggestions that nothing had happened. "You didn't get anything. Down deep inside you're still the same old Randy."

When I was younger, I had made several attempts to go to the altar to find salvation, but I was never real serious about it. I'd cry for a while and have an emotional experience until I felt better, only to remain in the same old rut. Today as a pastor, I have observed many people come to an altar of prayer only to receive what Pastor Ray Comfort refers to as a "horizontal salvation." They never have a real encounter with Jesus Christ. But when people have vertical encounters with Christ that go straight up between their souls and the Savior, it will change their lives forever.

When I walked away from that altar that night, I knew my life would never be the same. My spiritual eyes had been opened, and there was no doubt about it. My life had changed direction and was now traveling a different road, the straight and narrow road. And I wasn't looking back.

From then on, I was free to testify, and I often gave my testimony in church of how God had saved me. The Bible says in the book of Revelation that we will overcome Satan by the blood of the Lamb and the word of our testimony. I found out that the more I shared my testimony, the stronger I became. Sharing a public testimony is like injecting high-octane fuel into your spiritual tank.

At work, people knew that something had happened to me. I especially remember the next morning after my conversion. When I pulled into the ambulance station for duty, I parked my truck too close to the basketball hoop. One of my co-workers who enjoyed pushing my buttons immediately came out of the garage and began shooting hoops, allowing the ball to bounce off the roof of my truck. This normally would have been a no-no. If this same thing had happened just the day before, I would have grabbed him by the collar, shoved him up against the wall and threatened him within an inch of his life. I was proud of my truck, a Ford F-150 4x4 outfitted with a straight pipe, and I took good care of it.

But today, things were different. Although I may have looked at him in disgust, I had had a genuine encounter with the Savior and the Holy Spirit kept me silent, and I went into my office to begin work. And the next time I pulled into the parking lot, I made sure not to park under the basketball hoop.

No longer did I watch some of the filth that was on television or X-rated movies with the guys, nor did I participate in the obscene conversations that frequently took place. I'll never forget one day when someone said, "Randy, what's different about you?" Before I could get the answer out of my mouth, one of the other paramedics hollered out and said, "He's been saa-ved!" and threw his right hand up into the air.

When a person truly gets saved and gets the goods, people will know. You don't have to become a "Jesus freak" or a "Bible thumper" and get into people's faces. People will know that you're different by the way you live, act, and talk, and they'll be watching to see if you walk the walk, not just talk the talk. The Bible says that Christians will be known by their spiritual fruits.

As we left the campground that Wednesday night, I knew the road ahead would be tough. As the saying goes, God has not promised us a bed of roses, only a soft landing. My relationship with Trish and the family needed great mending. There would be many battles ahead, and I knew that Satan would declare all-out war. However, this time I didn't have to fight alone.

Not only is August 18 my physical birthday, it's also my spiritual birthday and the day the healing process began in my family.

The past twenty years have been unbelievable. Since the moment of my conversion, I have been overwhelmed at the countless lives God has allowed us to touch and the positive impact our family has had on numerous families across the country. Although we will never know the full spiritual impact we've had, we do know that the example our family has attempted to live may be the only Jesus that some people will ever see.

As I reflect on what God has done in our lives, it is not about me or anything we have done. It's all about Him. Only God has the power to take a mess like I presented to Him, fix it, and transform it into something that can be used for His glory. It boggles my mind to think that God could take a nobody and make him a somebody who can reach anybody.

If you put your faith and trust in Jesus and allow Him to save you and change your life, your life will be like Vern Jackson's song that says,

> *"Higher than I've ever been*
> *Higher than yesterday's sin*
> *Where eagles can't soar*
> *I can see Heaven's door*
> *I'm flying higher than I've ever been."*

CHAPTER 13

The Music Begins

It was September of 1993, barely a month after God saved me. Trish and I were on our way home from attending a free-enterprise weekend with the Amway Corporation in Hershey, Pennsylvania. We'd had a wonderful weekend, having had the opportunity to hear speakers including Dr. Robert Schuler, the founder of the Crystal Cathedral in California, and John McCormack, the author of "Self-Made in America." We were fired up.

I remember Dr. Schuler using an acrostic of the word "strive," and the crux of his speech was going for your goals, dreams, and ambitions with gusto. Little did I know how important that speech would be to me as I, too, would have to strive with all my might to pursue the path that God was soon to open.

We had already been recognized at two rallies for attaining our first pin level. There was no doubt about it—I knew how to do this business, and it was growing. They said we were diamonds in the rough, and by now, I was beginning to believe it.

However, after the rally concluded that night, something changed in my heart.

On the way home, there wasn't much traffic as we headed east on the Pennsylvania Turnpike. Trish was tired and decided to lie down in the back of the van, and as I drove, the Lord began to speak to me. Somehow, within the depths of my soul, I knew that God had a much bigger plan for my life than drawing circles or doing CPR.

During the seminar that weekend, a great deal of time was spent focusing on our dreams. As I look back, it's hard for me to believe that just moments before we left the seminar, I was one of the guys standing on my seat in the stadium, hooting and hollering, "Fired up! Fired up!" As the miles clicked by, the Lord dealt with me about my dreams and what my heart's desire really was. I remembered my early childhood love of music and the desire to be in ministry.

From as early as I can remember, I had a consuming passion for music. As I drove, I remembered back to the first time I sang in church at the age of two, and later, to the time when I played my trumpet in church. Then I remembered the years spent taking piano, voice, and drum lessons. Although I didn't know it then, God was preparing me for a time such as this.

Through the silence, it was as if I could hear that still, small voice of the Holy Spirit saying, "Randy, the dreams of your colleagues in business are not your dreams. They are not what I have planned for your life." It was then that I knew without a doubt what I was supposed to do.

A few miles later, I hollered back and asked Trish if she was awake, and she said she was. She asked me how I was doing staying awake, and I said I was doing fine. Then I said, "Trish, the dreams of becoming rich, being diamonds, and having lots of material things are not my dreams. They are the dreams of our associates."

"What are your dreams?" she asked. I was quick to reply. "I'm going to have to sing and share the testimony of what God has done for me and how He has brought healing and restoration to our family."

My wife's answer was simple. "Well, what are you waiting for?"

Thus, our musical ministry journey began. And as quickly as we had jumped into the Amway business, we jumped right back out. God had given us a new vision.

After returning home, I knew if I was going to do what God wanted me to do, I should start looking for sound equipment and a keyboard. This went against every aspect of common sense. I was $30,000 in debt from misuse of credit cards, vehicle purchases, and selfishness, had no keyboard player, and didn't have one singing engagement booked. And yet, I was looking for sound equipment? I'm sure there are those who questioned my sanity.

By the way, I have figured out it's a normal reaction for people to question your sanity when you're doing what God wants you to do. Isaiah 55 says in verse 8, "'For my thoughts are not your thoughts and neither are your ways My ways,' saith the Lord. 'For as the heavens are higher than the earth, so are My ways higher than your ways, and My thoughts than your thoughts.'"

A few days later, I found myself at Osiecki Brothers Music in Erie, Pennsylvania. I knew a guy by the name of Walt Slivinski who worked there. I said, "Walt, I've been seriously thinking about getting into music ministry. Do you think it's possible that I could get a sound system and keyboard at a reasonable price?" He said, "Sure."

As I began to see some of the prices, I realized this was probably not going to happen, especially not with all the debt hanging over my head. But in spite of my doubts, we continued to look anyway.

He showed me a brand new Roland KR650 digital piano. It was awesome. I was drooling all over it like I had just been handed a piece of chocolate cherry cake. It had all the bells and whistles, all the latest technology including a floppy drive, and a sequencer. I think it had everything but the kitchen sink. We looked at speakers, stands, mics, cables, a mixer and everything else we would need to set up in a church for a concert.

Now get this: The keyboard alone listed for $4,700. The speakers were $500 apiece. And the actual retail price of the whole package would end up around $8,000. I didn't have that kind of money! I was broke.

Then I did a bold thing. A little bit of my Uncle Gary had rubbed off on me. I said, "Walt, this equipment is going to be used for the Lord for ministry. I only have so much money to spend. Could you present this to Harry Osiecki and see if he would be willing to cut me a deal on this? You tell him what we will be using it for and make him an offer. You tell him if he can sell me the whole package for one penny under $5,000, I'll buy it."

Walt just looked at me with a blank stare and laughed. "Randy, I know Mr. Osiecki. He's never going to do that."

Well, call it a miracle or just that he was eager to make a sale. I call it a God thing. Walt went into the back and talked to Harry Osiecki and returned with a smile on his face. He said, "Randy, you got your price. He'll let you have your package for forty-nine, ninety-nine, ninety-nine!"

I said, "You're kidding me! He's going to do it?"

The next thing I did was really stupid. I had the audacity to ask Walt if he could hold that equipment for two weeks while I thought about it. What a stupid thing!

Walt said he would do his best to hold the equipment, but wasn't sure how long they would be able to honor that price. We left anyway. I had put a fleece out and was too blind to see it.

On the way home, I called my dad and told him about the offer of $4,999.99. By this time, Dad and I were rebuilding our broken relationship, and I was beginning to place some trust in him again. Dad said, "I don't know, son. Maybe you better be a little careful." Dad always erred on the side of caution. Years of experience had taught him to approach things sensibly. "Are you sure you want to do this? Are you sure God wants you to do this?"

I said, "Yeah, Dad, I really think this is what God is calling me into. But I'm not sure if I should go into debt for the purchase."

Years later, at one of our concerts, Dad told me, "Son, I'm sure glad you made the decision to buy that equipment." He was proud of what our family was doing.

Needless to say, the next two weeks were agony. I couldn't stand it any longer. So I called Walt and asked him if he still had the equipment for the same price. He said yes, and I was on my way to Erie to do what I should have done two weeks earlier.

Okay, so now I had all this fancy equipment. What was I going to do with it? The fact was that most people had never heard of Randy Keeling. I had never gone to Bible college, nor had I ever formally studied music. And I was naïve enough to think that I was going to get a phone call with an invitation to do a concert? Yeah, right.

It was the end of September of 1993 when we got our equipment, and all through the month of October, we rehearsed and located a keyboard player, all the while wondering what we were going to do with all this equipment. We had to pay for it, and I was eager to get started. But how?

Then it happened. I got a phone call from a guy in Franklin, Pennsylvania, who had heard that I was starting a music ministry. He wanted to know if I would come to their church in November for an interdenominational youth rally and share my testimony and sing.

The rest is history. We did our first concert in November of 1993. Our kids were very small. I'll never forget that night, Jeff getting up and coming over and singing a song with me. He was just a little guy. A couple of the songs I sang that night included "When He Was on the Cross, I Was on His Mind," and "When the Savior Reached Down for Me." These were songs that I performed often in the early years.

I can't remember many of the details of the concert other than the fact that God revealed to me in a new way that this was His plan for my life. The concert was a success, the people liked it, and we were called back to minister to that congregation several times. What would become known as The Keelings began that night in Franklin.

When I started, it was mostly a solo ministry. Glenna Guntrum from Rimersburg was my first keyboard player. She was a good evangelistic-style player and traveled with us for nearly three and a half years, during which God started opening many doors. We sang at nursing homes, churches, civic clubs, and dinners. We sang anywhere they would have us. I would have played a concert for barnyard animals had they been able to call and invite us. I think you get the message. I loved music.

About two years into the ministry, we invited John and Debbie Neely to join our ministry team. They traveled with us for six and a half years. We sang trios together, and John and I sang with two other gentlemen who had joined the group, Mark Miller and Tim Troyer. Together, we four men made up the group called Solid Rock Old-Time Gospel Quartet. John was a great guitar player, and he and Debbie knew their harmony. I have not met many people who can hold their harmony parts as well as they could. By this time, we were singing two or three times most weekends.

As they say, all good things must come to an end, and Glenna informed us that she needed to resign at the end of 1996. We were grateful for her service, and she had done a great job, but now we had to move on and search for a new keyboard player. We were introduced to Jeremy Sommers from Hartville, Ohio, and after a tryout, Jeremy came on board. He was an excellent musician and brought a Southern Gospel style of playing to our music. During the week, Jeremy attended Malone College in Canton, Ohio where he was majoring in piano performance. He was with us for about three years and became just like a son. I really appreciated him then and still do to this day.

As our kids continued to mature, so did their musical talents. In our concerts, we began involving them more and more. My ultimate dream was to finally reach the day when my kids could stand in the gap and take a vital role in our ministry. When the time came for the Neelys to resign, amazingly, we never missed a beat. The kids were ready and took their places at my side.

We were singing in the Youth Tabernacle in Stoneboro Camp and Jeremy Sommers, who was supposed to meet us there, never showed up. We found out later he was sitting on I-76 in a major traffic jam, with no cell phone or any way of notifying us that he couldn't make it to the service. All we knew was we had no keyboard player. It was a helpless feeling. Now what do we do?

I had no choice. It was time to have a conversation with my son Jeff. We had been featuring Jeff on piano solos in our concerts, but he had not yet played for congregational singing. He was good at playing by ear but he was still having difficulty reading music. The service would start in ten minutes. I frantically explained the situation to Jeffrey and said, "This is your time. I need you now. Do or die, sink or swim. Jeremy's not going to be able to be here with us. You're up. It's your time." And willingly or not, he did it. And he did it well.

Up until then, Jeffrey had been our bass guitar player. But now, at the age of thirteen, he became our full-time keyboard player. With each successive concert he played, he became better and better, and more confident. I don't say this just because Jeffrey is my son, but he is everything that any Gospel group could ever dream of in a keyboard player. During the sixteen years that he has been playing, he has grown and developed into one of the best Gospel pianists in the country in my opinion. At many of our concerts, people come up to me and say, "Anthony Burger lives on through your son." As a side note, Jeff spent much time listening to Anthony play and held him in high regard.

Doug, the kid in the middle, soon stepped up to become our bass player, and Lynn, our youngest, took her role as our tenor singer. The pieces were falling into place. With Trish working behind the scenes and helping with songwriting, we truly became a full-time family music ministry.

At the peak of our ministry in 2006, 2007 and 2008, we were singing 120 or more dates per year and had recorded fifteen albums, two of which were produced by Roger Talley of the Talley Trio, and Greg Shockley, formerly of The Singing Americans. Under their direction, we released our first two radio singles, two original songs, "Old Fashioned" and "Walkin' with the Lord." Both songs were added to the playlists of numerous radio stations across the country that played Southern Gospel music.

In 2006, our family was invited to perform during the jam session along with Christian comedian Tim Lovelace at the National Quartet Convention in Louisville, Kentucky. What a great experience, one we will never forget.

In January of 2006, we launched *Southern Praise*, a weekly half-hour radio broadcast featuring some of the best in Southern and classic Gospel music. At its peak, *Southern Praise* was heard on 22 stations as far west as Omack, Washington; as far south as Dadeville, Alabama, and around the world on Internet radio.

In October of 2006, we recorded our first live concert DVD, *Center Stage*. The project was recorded in front of an audience of more than 1,000 at the First Church of God, now known as New Beginnings Church of God, in Meadville.

In the spring of 2008 and in honor of our fifteen-year anniversary, I released my first solo project, *One Heart, One Soul, One Voice*. The title song from that project, "Where No One Stands Alone," was released to radio via RadioActive Airplay and debuted at No. 12 on the Top 100 Gospel Chart, then rose to No. 7 and held there for two weeks. It never made it to No. 1, but as I said previously, it's not about us. It's about Him, and just the fact that we had made it into the Top 10 was good enough for me.

Another highlight came in March of 2008. We were notified that our family had been nominated to receive the 2008 Keystone Award, which the Pennsylvania Southern Gospel Music Association gives annually to a Gospel group, duo, or soloist who has accomplished something outstanding for the cause of Christ during the past year. In the fall of 2008, we traveled to Chambersburg, Pennsylvania to receive the award and performed a concert that night, along with Gaither Homecoming Friend, Ivan Parker.

Our first No. 1 song came in the fall of 2008 after the release of *U-Turn*, our second album to be released that year in honor of our fifteen-year anniversary. "U-Turn" was the title song, a song that I wrote which was also released on the RadioActive Airplay charts. As an added benefit, we also had a No. 2 song, "The Golden Street," which I co-wrote with Charles Jarvis, the publisher of Tribune Chronicle daily newspaper in Warren, Ohio. These events were just added blessings along the way.

In 2007, our music ministry made a paradigm shift. In both 2005 and 2006, we attended the National Quartet Convention in Louisville, Kentucky, and as mentioned earlier, we had been invited to perform in the Saturday afternoon jam session with comedian Tim Lovelace. We were scheduled to return in 2007 and had already paid for our ten-by-ten space in the convention center, about $450.

However, something drastic happened during that year. While we were in Phoenix, Arizona, editing the DVD that was shot in the fall of 2006, we became aware of the infiltration and influences of the homosexual community in the field of Gospel music and in particular, Southern Gospel music.

After much research, fact-finding, soul searching, prayer and conversations with decision-makers in the Gospel music industry, we made the collective decision as a family to no longer pursue the dream of becoming a nationally known Southern Gospel group. Rather, we would honor God, stick to our convictions, and, if it meant the loss of bookings, we were going to do our best to raise a high standard and be the best that we could be regardless of what others did. With a new motto of *Integrity, Character, and Quality*, we forged ahead.

To my delight, we never missed a beat or lost a booking, and actually did better financially than we had ever done before. CD sales picked up and the demand for concert dates with The Keelings was higher than ever before. I believe that God honored us for being faithful to His word and the stand that we were taking against this abomination.

In October of 2009, we celebrated sixteen years with another concert at New Beginnings Church of God in Meadville. On our previous two projects, we worked with Gaither Homecoming Friend, former baritone singer with the Old Friends Quartet, and Dove Award winner, Wesley Pritchard, as our vocal coach, and a wonderful orchestrator and arranger from Fayetteville, North Carolina, Milton Smith. At our invitation, Wesley Pritchard came to help us celebrate sixteen years of The Keelings.

When he arrived at the church and saw a thousand seats set up, he said, "Randy, what other groups are singing with you tonight?" And I replied, "Just The Keelings."

I asked Wesley, "How many songs are you planning to sing?" He said, "One. I only came with one. I came to hear The Keelings. I have heard about you, and I want to see what you guys do in person." I knew in my mind that he was questioning whether or not the little group called The Keelings, from Hadley, Pennsylvania, could draw a thousand people.

At 6:00 o'clock when the doors opened, there was a line of people waiting to get in, from the sanctuary doors all the way through the lobby, all the way out to the outside. At about 6:30, Wesley asked Jeff, "How many people were you expecting tonight?" Jeff answered, "Oh, we have over a thousand tickets out for this event." I knew he still didn't believe it was going to happen.

But at 7:00 p.m. when the concert started, nearly every seat in the house was filled. Wesley said, "Randy, I don't know what you're doing or how you do it, but don't stop." He told me of concerts of nationally known groups that he had attended that would never be able to draw a crowd like our little group had. I was humbled by this and thanked the Lord for the decision we had made to honor Him.

One thing I have learned is, what will draw people to the Lord the most is transparency. When the smoke clears from all the "dog-and-pony shows," and when the hype has faded away, what people really long to see onstage is a group that has a genuine, sincere love for the Lord. Over the years, The Keelings have done their utmost to be as transparent and genuine as we can possibly be. Our desire is to be the same offstage as we were onstage. We do not want to be Christians only on Sunday; we want to live it Monday through Saturday as well.

Today, we are in the process of trying to downsize our music ministry with the family getting older, the kids starting their own lives and having kids of their own, and my expanding responsibilities now as a church pastor. Instead, our music ministry continues to grow. Every year when I look at the bottom line, even though we sang fewer concerts, we come out the same or ahead financially. And the demand for concerts continues to come with new opportunities. The kids have all grown up, and my son-in-law is now singing with the group. Our first grandson was born July 30, 2012, and at the age of forty-eight, I can hardly wait to see what will be coming next for The Keelings. In my heart, I know the best is yet to come.

CHAPTER 14

Death Route

Just because you have an encounter with Christ and are forgiven doesn't mean for a moment that your battles and temptations are over. It's actually quite the contrary.

Most often, when you make a move toward God, all hell will break loose. Satan's battleground is your mind. I heard one preacher say that the only time the devil cares anything about you is when he starts to lose control over you. If he has you, it doesn't matter. But just wait until he starts to lose his grip.

The Apostle Paul says in Ephesians 6:12, "For we wrestle not against flesh and blood, but against principalities, against powers, against the rulers of the darkness of this world, against spiritual wickedness in high places. Therefore take unto you the whole armor of God, that ye may be able to withstand in the evil day and having done all to stand."

One of the drastic mistakes new Christians often make is failing to immerse themselves in the Word of God and remain vigilant. Too often, they jump onto Easy Street, coasting along, never realizing that danger is around the corner. In my experience as a Christian, I have never found Easy Street. You have to work hard at it every day and make a conscious choice daily to serve the Lord.

A pastor friend of mine gave me a copy of the *Screwtape Letters* written by C.S. Lewis. I would encourage you to read it. It will give you a vivid description of how the devil and his demonic associates connive and scheme to break down a man or woman. The devil is the master deceiver and faithfully studies his prey. He knows which buttons to push.

I wish I could say that after I accepted Christ, I never stumbled again. But an alcoholic or smoker trying to break his or her addiction often relapses for short periods until he gets his act together and is strong enough to overcome his addiction. The same is true for the individual struggling with a sexual addiction, or any addiction, for that matter.

There is no doubt that I got saved that night at the old camp meeting, but newborn babies never hit the ground running. Usually they will stumble and fall several times before they learn to walk and then to run.

About a year and a half before my conversion, I had developed a strong physical and psychological relationship with another individual. At one point, I had seriously considered getting an apartment and moving in with her as I mentioned in a previous chapter. On the night of my conversion, I thought I had let go of her emotionally. I was finally over her—or so I thought. Unfortunately, she was not as willing as I was to let go.

The amount of power and sway she held over me was unbelievable. When I look back, I remember her eyes and the way she spoke to me. I belonged to her, and she wasn't about to let go without a real fight. Talk about a living hell—it was like I was living in a nightmare that wouldn't end.

By now you can only imagine the roller coaster ride that my wife, Trish, was on. She had already been hurt deeply and didn't deserve to go through this again.

The other woman was relentless. She wouldn't give up. She called my office, my cell phone and made hundreds of hang-up calls to our home. As the battle raged, I felt myself beginning to weaken. She was wearing me down, and as much as I wanted to remain faithful to my wife, I felt myself beginning to fall back into that same old me, the one I hated.

The Apostle Paul gives a vivid description in Romans 7 of the war between the flesh and the spirit that takes place in a man, and that war was raging in my life. I was again at another crisis point in my life and was presented with two choices: Would I beg God for His help and surrender to Him, or would I allow the devil to win and sink back into the old life that I had been delivered from?

I was desperate, on one side being pulled by a wife who truly loved me and was willing to sacrifice or do anything to keep me on the right track, and on the other side being pulled by another woman who was hell-bent on keeping me in her grasp.

By now Trish was involved, and on one occasion she actually went with me for a face-to-face encounter with this person, as together we tried to make the madness go away. No matter what we did, the harassment continued.

I'll never forget the day Trish called me to inform me that the other woman was driving her truck up and down the road in front of our house. I immediately left the office and headed for home.

Being concerned for the safety of Trish and the kids, I had purchased a small, semi-automatic pistol for Trish. I remember telling Trish, "If that woman attempts to come through the door or tries to do anything crazy, call the state police and fire the gun at her until she's down." When I arrived home, the little gray truck was nowhere to be seen. However, when I entered the house, I found Trish standing behind the door with the gun in one hand and a phone in the other. There's no doubt in my mind that she would have pulled the trigger that day.

On the surface, I tried to be upbeat and keep a positive face about the situation. But I must admit that during this time, my faith was faltering. I knew that God had done a wonderful work that night in August of 1993, and I knew without a doubt that He had called me into ministry. By now, we were singing several concerts a month, and it seemed like God was beginning to bless our family.

However, behind the scenes and deep within my soul the battle raged. The devil was making one last-ditch effort to drag me into the pit again. And he was using this other woman to do it.

Looking back, it's very clear to me now that I was mostly to blame. I recognize the fact now that I hadn't let go of her. Matthew 5:29-30 says if your right hand offends you, cut it off, or if your right eye offends you, pluck it out. Of course, we would not literally do that. However, in a spiritual sense, if you want to kill a snake, you've got to cut the head off, which I had never done. Sometimes I'm not sure what I was thinking. Maybe I enjoyed her attention, or maybe I just wanted to hold on to a little bit of the past. But it's obvious to me now that I still hadn't made the final surrender.

During this time, I learned a very important lesson about God: Just like an earthly father who is patient and loving toward his children, all the more is our Heavenly Father patient and loving toward His. He loves us unconditionally. Romans 6:6 says, "Knowing this, that our old man is crucified with Him, that the body of sin might be destroyed, that henceforth we should not serve sin." The problem was that I had never crucified the old man. He was alive and well.

The breakthrough to victory started while I was away from home at an EMS conference in Harrisburg, Pennsylvania. It was a three-day conference, and you can only imagine the temptations. I was under horrific attack from the enemy.

Before I continue, let me stop right here and say what I have said at hundreds of concerts, "Without God, we are nothing and without God in our lives, we can do nothing."

By the evening of the first day of the conference, I felt as though my world was crumbling all around me. Sometimes we have to allow our children to feel some pain in order to get their attention, and I believe that is what was happening to me that night. I remember burying my head in the pillow and crying myself to sleep.

By the afternoon of the second day, I was a mess. Down deep in my heart, I did not want to fall back into the old lifestyle, one filled with guilt and remorse. But I am human; my flesh was weak, and the temptation was overwhelming. I knew if something didn't change, I was destined to fall again.

Between seminar sessions, I went back to my room and threw myself across the hotel bed. I felt so alone. Trish wasn't there to help me. I was on my own, just me and God and the overwhelming temptation I was facing. In desperation, I threw myself on the mercy of God and once again, I started to get real honest with my Heavenly Father.

As I lay there, I picked up the Bible that was in my room and started reading randomly. Thank God for the Gideons who place Bibles in hotels across the country and around the world. The Bible opened to Psalms 91 and I began to read:

"Surely He shall deliver thee from the snare of the fowler, and from the noisome pestilence. He shall cover thee with his feathers, and under His wings shalt thou trust: His truth shall be thy shield and buckler. Thou shalt not be afraid for the terror by night; nor for the arrow that flieth by day; nor for the pestilence that walketh in darkness; nor for the destruction that wasteth at noonday."

In the same chapter, the Lord said, "'Because he hath set his love upon me, therefore will I deliver him: I will set him on high, because he hath known my name. He shall call upon me, and I will answer him: I will be with him in trouble; I will deliver him, and honor him. With long life will I satisfy him, and shew him my salvation.'"

As I read these verses, it was as if I could hear the voice of God saying, "Randy, you're not alone. I'm here with you." Afresh and anew, I could feel His presence as it surrounded me. I felt warm, and my skin tingled. It was as if I had been reborn all over again.

After reading those words, my confidence and faith in the Lord were renewed. With the Lord at my side, together we could face anything. Not only had my spiritual mind been awakened, but my creative mind as well. As I lay there on the bed that afternoon, the words to a new song started to flow. I picked up a pad of paper and wrote:

> *"There are some times when I feel*
> *I just can't make it on my own*
> *There are times when I feel all alone*
> *That's when Jesus in His love*
> *Gently pulls me to His side, and He whispers,*
> *'You're Never Alone.'*
>
> *For He's a friend beyond compare*
> *Every burden he will share*
> *He'll pick me up, should I fall along the way*
> *He'll never forsake me through it all*
> *He's never too busy when I call*
> *Since I found Jesus*
> *I'm never alone."*

Not only did God give me another verse, but he gave me the tune to go along with the words. Later in 1995, we recorded the song and titled it, *Never Alone.*

A preacher friend of mine once gave an illustration that makes a lot of sense. He said, "If you own a house and a window's broken, you don't tear down the whole house just to repair the broken window. You fix the window and move on." My spiritual house had a broken window, and Jesus, the Master Repairman, had just started the process of replacing the broken window of my spiritual house that afternoon in Harrisburg.

The struggle that had raged like a roaring lion ended like a meek lamb. By the time we got to the summer of 1995, the battle was much less intense, but there were still times when the beast would rear its ugly head. One afternoon while sitting in my office, I began to pray earnestly for direction and guidance for my future. I wanted to be free of all reminders of the past, and most of all, I didn't want any more harassment from past associations. I was fed up with it and I wanted to be free. Something drastic needed to be done.

As I prayed, again I could hear the voice of God as He gently said, "Randy, how serious are you about wanting freedom? What would you be willing to do?" As I pondered this, the thought came to my mind, "Would you be willing to quit your job?"

Believe you me, when I said I would be willing to do anything, this was not what I had in mind. By now I had been promoted and was director of marketing and public relations for the Pennsylvania division of Rural/Metro Ambulance. In addition to that, I held the position of float supervisor on weekends and was making $40,000 a year, plus benefits, and finally, after much struggle, was able to support my family pretty well. I really needed the job. And the money was even subsidizing our ministry.

However, more than a job, money or material things, I wanted to please God. I wanted freedom. When I called Trish to tell her of my decision, she said, "Are you sure about this?" I replied, "Never been more sure about anything in my life."

When I turned in my two-week notice, I walked in and told the general manager I was resigning. He said, "Randy, you're crazy. You'll be hard-pressed to find another setup as sweet as the one you have now."

He asked me, "What are you going to do if the job up in Meadville you're leaving here for falls through?" And rather flippantly, I replied, "Well, if I lose my job in Meadville, I'll get up the next morning and my wife will ask me if I want eggs for breakfast. I'll say yes, and she'll fix me my eggs, and life will go on."

More than twenty years have passed since I walked out of the office of Rural/Metro Ambulance in Greenville. The phone calls stopped, as did the harassment, and we have never seen nor heard anything from the individual who couldn't let go. I had finally stepped up to the plate and made the decision to kill the old man within me, to cut off the head of the snake that was destroying me. No matter what my future would hold from here on out, I would focus my attention only on God and my family.

When you get desperate and ask God for change, be aware of what you ask for. The change may not be to remove something from your life as I had thought. It may be that *you* have to be removed in order to see change come. Sometimes you need to have the courage to do the hard thing.

To this day, I can truly say that God has taken care of us every step of the way. Looking back, the decision I made to walk away from a good job, although at the time it seemed to fly in the face of logic and common sense, was one of the best decisions I've ever made.

The battle was over. I was finally *free!*

CHAPTER 15

Clueless

One of the greatest blessings a man can have is his children, and God gave me three of the most wonderful kids in the world whom I love dearly. There was a time when I was clueless about my role and responsibility as a father, and regretfully, I often shirked my duty.

You can imagine the readjustment that took place in our home after I became a Christian. My spiritual eyes were opened, and not only was God bringing healing between my wife and me, but at the same time I was accepting the challenges of being a father. Talk about a fumble-futz! I made a real mess of it. I've often wondered why our government, which mandates everything else, doesn't make people take parenting classes. I'd make an awesome teacher, as I have graduated with honors from Hard Knocks University.

I'll never forget when my first son was born. I was working a shift on the ambulance and had just brought a patient into the Greenville Hospital emergency room. When we arrived, two of my co-EMTs met me in the ER and told me they'd received a call from my wife. "It's time."

I hurried home, and Trish and I got into the car and headed for Kittanning. We were living in Worthington at the time we found out she was pregnant but had since moved about seventy miles away to Clarks Mills, Pennsylvania because of my employment. Her doctor, Dr. Keith Buck, had his office in Kittanning and worked out of Armstrong County Memorial Hospital. (In a recent conversation, I found out that Dr. Buck delivered 9,163 babies during his career.)

Just a few days before, we had been to the doctor's office, and he said that the baby was still in a high position, and we should come back in about three weeks because we lived so far away. Now, here we were again, only this time we went directly to the hospital. They checked Trish out and said, "You're still not ready. The baby has not dropped."

Common sense prevailed, and we elected to stay at my parents' place in Worthington due to the distance. All through the rest of that day, Trish's pains intensified. The interesting thing about it was that all her labor pains were in her back.

At 11:30 p.m., out of frustration, not knowing what to do, we trotted off to the hospital again, only for them to send us back home another time. By this time, the contractions were very intense, but they insisted that the baby was not ready to come and we should go back home.

At 3:00 a.m., we returned to the hospital due to the intense labor pain. Somehow, they just could not seem to get it into their heads that this baby wanted out! We were told the same old thing—go back home and wait.

Trish couldn't lie down. She could hardly walk. She couldn't sit. This was a terrible predicament. Phew! Sure glad I'm a man. Thankfully, I'll never have to experience that. I tried to make her as comfortable as possible, propping her up with blankets and pillows, and padding every part I could, thinking in my mind, "Is the sun ever going to shine again?"

This kid was being *real* stubborn, a pattern he would follow throughout his life!

About 9:30 the next morning, out of sheer frustration, we trudged to the hospital for the fourth time. Dr. Buck was not available. He was at a dentist's appointment near Pittsburgh. By now the labor and delivery department knew they couldn't send us home as they had done several times before. We were going to camp out in their doorway until they did something.

Trish laid in the labor and delivery room until approximately 2:00 p.m., after having been in labor all night long. When Dr. Buck arrived, he was furious because they hadn't taken any action or notified him of our previous visits or our situation. He was immediately concerned that severe complications were pending and ordered an emergency C-section. "She's already been in labor for fourteen hours and she could lie here until the cows come home. But it's obvious this baby is not coming out the way it's supposed to."

Within minutes, she was prepped and rushed to surgery, where a C-section was performed. Jeffrey was born on January 11, 1985—within the first year of our marriage—and checked in at seven pounds, ten ounces. Wow! What a feeling! I was a dad, but I didn't have a clue about how to be one.

I'll never forget holding Jeffrey for the first time. The nurse asked if I'd like to see him and I said, "Yes!" Trish was still in the recovery room and was not able to be with me. I don't know if they still practice this today, but they placed him in my arms, and I was allowed to feed him a bottle of sugar water. He was a cute little bugger. I remember looking at his little fingers and toes. *Man!* If only I knew what to do next. I was nineteen and barely out of diapers myself, and here I was with this little guy in my arms.

I've told Jeffrey several times that he is responsible for initiating winter in 1985. The day we brought him home from the hospital was the day that winter started. It had hardly snowed in December, but now, in January, on the way home to Hadley from the hospital, we were driving in one of the worst blizzards imaginable. It was snowing and blowing. There were cars in the ditches, and we were just creeping along.

After we got Jeffrey home, we soon got back into a routine—I worked, and Trish took care of the baby. Up until this time, I had been faithful to my wife. And at a time when our relationship should have been getting stronger and when I should have been focusing on my responsibilities, the demons of my past were starting to get restless, which contributed to my downward spiral.

The reality of responsibility hit me hard. I was young, immature, and terrible at making decisions. We needed money, so I started to work day and night in order to make ends meet. Instead of drawing closer as a family, we started drifting apart, in large part due to the fact that I was never home. Over the years, I have never been afraid to try my hand at anything if it would bring extra income into the family, from flipping pizzas to digging ditches or driving trucks. You name it; if we were hungry and needed the money, I did it. Times were hard, and the holes needed to be plugged.

At about the same time that my life was spiraling out of control, we found out that Trish was pregnant again. During the nineteenth week of her pregnancy, we received a phone call from Dr. Buck telling us that the alpha fetal protein (AFP) test came back too high. He wanted us to go to West Penn Hospital in Pittsburgh for a Level 2 ultrasound. Although I was an EMT at the time, I wasn't an expert in the field of obstetrics. I asked Dr. Buck why this test would be needed and he said, "Well, there is a real chance that this baby could have spina bifida. If the baby has this complication, the $64,000 question would be what to do next."

On the appointed day, we traveled to Pittsburgh for the procedure, and to our amazement, we found out the reason for the high AFP levels—we were having twins! We were all worked up for nothing. Now we just had to figure out what we were going to do with two more instead of one. And how were we going to afford this?

They videotaped both of the fetuses and were pretty certain they were boys. At nineteen weeks, they appeared healthy and their development was on schedule. My wife was excited, and I was trying to be an excited expectant father, but just couldn't quite get there because of the life I was secretly leading.

Twins. Our families were very familiar with twins. Both my mother and Trish's mother are identical twins. And at the same time we were expecting twins, my wife's first cousin Karen was carrying a set of twins. We were popping them out like rabbits. Combined, there are 17 sets of twins on both sides of our families. My daughter-in-law, Hannah, who is married to Jeff—her mother is an identical twin. My poor kids, if the tradition continues.

August 7, 1987, was the scheduled date for the birth of our twin boys. Trish would be having another C-section. The doctor decided that it would be too risky for Trish to attempt a natural delivery because of the chance of complications. As we anticipated the birth of the twins, we decided that their names would be Douglas Eugene and Darren Edward, both named for the initials of my dad, Dan E. Keeling.

About three days before we went to the hospital, Trish told me she felt a violent kick on her lower left side. She said, "The baby on the lower left side felt like it wanted to kick my guts out." I think in retrospect what she was feeling was a desperate attempt by that baby to survive.

They were fraternal twins. Doug weighed in at seven pounds, fourteen ounces and was a healthy, robust baby boy. Darren, the one who was situated on the left side, weighed in at only four pounds, fifteen ounces. Darren was born with a faint heartbeat but never breathed on his own.

While resuscitative measures were being performed, Dr. Buck grabbed me and took me into a back room. He showed me a blue surgical towel that contained sections of the umbilical cords from both babies. "Randy, you're in the emergency field. Can you tell me what's wrong with this picture?" One was pink and very normal looking. You could see that the blood supply through this cord had been well oxygenated, and the blood was red. However, the second cord was twisted and the blood was purple, a sign of oxygen starvation and fetal distress.

Dr. Buck said they were trying to stabilize Darren, and if they succeeded, did they have my permission to transport him to Children's Hospital in Pittsburgh? Why did he have to ask? Just do it.

Unfortunately, Darren was never able to be revived, and that afternoon, after living only about an hour in this world, another little angel went home to be with Jesus. Our ways are not God's ways. It's now obvious to me that God needed this little guy in Heaven with Him more than Trish and I would need him down here.

It seemed surreal standing there in the nursery beside my two baby boys, one who was kicking and healthy and doing well and the other who lay lifeless. How is one supposed to feel during this time? You're happy and yet you're sad.

While Trish was still in the recovery room, they told her that Darren didn't make it. This was obviously going to be much harder on her than it would be on me as she had carried him full term. As a man, it is difficult for me to comprehend a mother's love for her children, but somehow, deep in my heart, I truly believe that a bond between a mother and her children begins long before she ever feels the first sign of movement.

When they brought Trish back to her room, they brought both boys in for her and me to see. I'll never forget the look on her face as she held Doug for the first time. She was happy. And then they brought Darren in. She just held Darren in her arms and wept.

Later that afternoon, I was left with the task of making funeral arrangements. I went to Flick's Funeral Home in Worthington. Believe me, picking out a casket for your own flesh and blood at the age of twenty-one is not a task I would wish on anyone.

On the day we brought Doug home from the hospital, a small graveside service was performed that afternoon at the Presbyterian Cemetery in Worthington. Rev. Bob Hales, a great man of God, performed a short service for Darren. It was strange standing beside that little white casket, and yet we took comfort in our living son.

I've often wondered—and Trish and I have even talked about this—could it have been possible for Doug and Darren to communicate with each other as they were developing side by side in the womb? Somehow, I think this happened.

Doug was a special kid, the cuddly kind. When he hugs you, it's almost like being hugged by a big ol' teddy bear. When he was a kid, he loved his stuffed bears and always talked to them in his teddy bear voice.

Although it's not very noticeable today, Doug was born with a small birthmark on the left side of his head. Trish and I believe that this mark came as a result of his head being pressed up against his brother's, a living reminder of a brother who is in Heaven.

When we found out we were having twins, Trish decided to have a tubal ligation as we weren't planning on having any more children. However, in light of what had just happened and at the suggestion of Dr. Buck, we made the decision not to proceed with that surgery.

Almost three years later, on July 2, 1990, Little Miss Muffet, our daughter Lynn, was born. Coincidentally, she was born on the same date as my sister Connie who passed away in 1981. Lynn's birth brought healing to Trish and put a bright spot in the lives of my mom and dad. They now had something good to think about when Connie's birthday came around each year.

So here I was, twenty-four years old, a wife, two boys and a baby girl. I was numb, running hard, and living a crazy life. When I was at home, I tried to make sure that I spent some time with the kids, and I wanted them to know I loved them. But I must admit that many of the things that happened during their childhoods are nothing more than a blur because of my lack of attention, distractions, and restlessness, a regret I will carry with me to my grave.

In the early days, Jeffrey was a smart little bugger, sharp as a tack. I've often told Trish that Jeffrey got his strong will from her side of the family, but somehow I think I made a heavy contribution to that as well. Nowadays, I would probably be arrested for child abuse, as spanking seems to be old school. However, I remember reading something in the Bible where it says spare the rod, spoil the child.

Jeffrey was a real test of our patience. If he decided to throw a tantrum, we knew it was going to last for a while. You could stand him in the corner, yell at him, spank him, take toys away from him, and no matter what, he just wouldn't quit until he was ready. He was one of the most strong-willed kids I'd ever seen. This didn't set well with me as I was working most of the time. When I was home, it was important for me to get a little sleep. There were a few nights that he just wouldn't go to sleep, standing up in his crib and crying, crying, *crying*. We'd lay him back down and tell him he had to go to bed. But seconds later, he'd be right back up again.

Unfortunately, the boy took some serious spankings from me. It was a battle of the wills. He wouldn't give in, and I wouldn't give up. At times, Trish was just about out of her mind. She would turn to me in exasperation. "I don't know what to do with this kid."

On one occasion I remember his driving me to the point of utter frustration. It was time for him to take a nap, and as usual, he refused. We put him down, and within seconds, he was crying and climbing out of the crib. We put him back in the crib and he popped out like toast in a toaster. We spanked him and put him back in his crib. And he was back out. He just plain refused to give in and lie down.

Finally, I decided to let him stand in his crib and scream. This went on for 45 minutes or more, and he worked himself into a soaking-wet-with-sweat frenzy, holding his breath and then screaming at the top of his lungs. The kid wouldn't listen to reason. I had just come off a 24-hour shift that morning and wasn't in the mood to deal with this. He had both Trish and I about out of our minds.

Finally, in my frustration, I said, "All right, I'm going to cool you down."

I took him to the bathroom, where I put the plug in the bathtub and put about four inches of cold water in the bottom. He was in a fit of rage. His face was beet red, and heat was radiating off his body, he was so angry.

When he realized what I was going to do, he started screaming for me to quit, and I said, "Nope, you're going to learn." I put him in the cold water, clothes and all. I just said, "You're going to sit in the cold water until you cool down."

Jeffrey was about three years old when this happened, and I'm sure some of you who are reading this book will say that this was excessive punishment. But one thing's for sure, I got his attention that day, and we never had to deal with that problem again. When he started throwing fits thereafter, all I had to do was threaten him with the cold water. He knew I'd do it, and he'd settle right down.

One of the problems with parents and children today is that parents often lack the willpower or stamina to outlast their children when it comes to discipline. When a child's will is not broken, he or she will rule the family. It is our responsibility as parents to see that our children come under subjection to our authority from a Biblical perspective.

Please understand, there is a difference between breaking a child's will versus breaking a child's spirit. Children will recover and love you more when their wills have been broken and they understand who the authority figure is in their lives. However, if you abuse them and break their spirits, they will resent you and carry bitterness and unneeded baggage into their adult lives.

Jesus commanded us in Matthew 5:37 to let our yea be yea and our nay be nay. Nothing irritates me more than to see parents who will tell their kids no, and then go back on their word within five minutes and give in. This is the point when I'd rather spank the parent than the child. Not only does it send the wrong message to your kids when you go back on your word, but it's lying.

This is just a little sermon I threw into the book. You can consider it a freebie.

Another thing that I did to punish the boys that I'm not proud of, was to threaten to take them to George Junior Republic, a juvenile detention center in Grove City, Pennsylvania, when they were spatting and scrapping with each other.

There were a couple of times in my frustration that I said, "Pack your bags, boys, I'm taking you to George Junior Republic." A few times I actually made them pack their clothes and put them in the car, and we headed off for Grove City. I remember on one occasion Doug said, "Dad, can I take my bear with me?" I said, "Yeah, you can take your bear."

We wouldn't get far down the road and the boys would be crying, *"Daddy, Daddy, please, please take us back home. We'll be good. We promise."* Most often, I would pull the vehicle over, turn around and say, "All right, but you've got to promise me you're not going to act that way again."

Today, I understand that was a stupid way to punish kids. I must admit that in my ignorance, I did that a couple times. But one thing's for sure, whether it was out of fear or respect, they started to listen. Had I been a little older and more mature, I'd have been able to handle things differently.

At this time, my secret life was consuming my attention. These were the early years, and I didn't know the first thing about parenting.

CHAPTER 16

Becoming a Dad

In retrospect, I now understand that during the times when I was running hard, Jeffrey badly needed his dad, but I was AWOL. Regretfully, there were also many times when I got really mad at him. His strong will made me angry, and my punishments were often severe, bordering on abuse.

Before I continue any further, let me stop here and say that Jeffrey has become an extraordinary young man. The strong will that he displayed as a child is now very prevalent in his adult life as a Christian. He is unwavering in his faith and commitment in his relationships with his God and his wife. I am proud to claim him as my son, and I love him. How our relationship survived is a miracle, but in my heart, I love him more today than I have words to express. Our bond is stronger than it's ever been. I would never want to consider life without my son.

After becoming a Christian, my spiritual understanding was awakened, and I began to take my responsibility as a father more seriously. Moms and dads, remember this: Your children are your gift from God. Laying aside all material wealth and cares of this world, the most important thing you can accomplish is to live a Christian life and set an example for your children.

Dads, it is your responsibility to bring out and nurture the masculinity in your boys. In your children's eyes, you are the godhead figure in the home. If you can teach them to love, respect, and obey you, they will be able to much more easily submit to, love, respect and honor their Heavenly Father.

Dads, it is also your responsibility to love and nurture and bring out the femininity in your daughters. As her father, you should be her first love and her hero. She should be able to trust you and know that you will be looking out for her wellbeing and her future.

If moms and dads could just grasp this concept, it would change our world one family at a time, and our children would have the desire to be Christians and duplicate it again with their children, so they would be able to spend eternity in Heaven. I have often said you can't take your money or your wealth with you when you leave this world. The only thing you can do is create an environment in your home that will increase your chances of taking your family with you, by living a godly example and making the things of God important in your home.

In our current world, many parents have their priorities upside down. When you have children, your first obligation must be to provide for and nurture them. However, today, a great number of parents are pursuing their own interests, neglecting their duties, and leaving the job of raising their children to the school system, the sitter, the television, and/or whatever electronic gizmo they can use to pacify and keep their children quiet.

An eye-opening wakeup call came on Thanksgiving Day of 1993, just three months after my conversion. I was still fighting the demons of the past, but attempting to accept the challenges of being a good husband and a Christian father. We were in serious debt and struggling financially because of bad financial decisions in the past. We were forced to save money anywhere we could. One way we could do this was for me to give the boys their haircuts and save on the expense of a barber. Believe me, I'm the last person you would want cutting your hair! I can make a mess of trimming my beard, let alone cutting someone else's hair.

Normally on Thanksgiving Day, we would travel to Rimersburg to Great-Grandpa Bowser's house for Thanksgiving dinner. However, on this day, Doug was sick which meant Trish, Lynn, and I would be staying at home. Trish's parents had invited Jeffrey to ride with them to Rimersburg for Thanksgiving dinner. But before he could go, he needed a haircut.

Jeffrey was always a fidgety little kid, always moving. So I took him back to the bathroom, stood him up on a chair in front of the mirror and stripped him down to his underwear. I cut a hole in a plastic garbage bag and put it over his head to keep the hair from getting all over him and began to cut his hair. By the way, if you're already hot and sweaty, putting a plastic bag on your bare skin only makes you sweat more. I used to do the dumbest things.

It's only natural that a kid's going to squirm. You get a scrawny, bony eight-year-old boy and tell him to hold still, and you know what he's going to do. Then, try cutting his hair, with it getting down underneath a hot, sweaty plastic bag. It's inevitable—it's going to itch. And he's going to wriggle and scratch.

I used to give Jeffrey a teddy bear haircut, sort of like a crew cut. The more he moved, the more upset I became. Finally I got to the point where I said, "If you move one more time, I am going to whip you, and you will not be allowed to go with Nan and Pa to Grandpa Bowser's today."

Well, the inevitable happened. You know what he did. He moved. And you know what I did. True to my word, I gave him a spanking and said, "That's it, you're not going. You're going to learn to listen to what I say." I felt that if I went back on my word, I would not be acting as a good father.

My punishment for Jeffrey started a series of negative reactions. Trish was upset with me for being unreasonable. Not only that, she had to call her parents to say that Jeffrey wasn't going with them. So now they were upset. Jeffrey was angry at me and feeling sad. But I wasn't about to budge. This was a matter of principle. Talk about making a mess of things. I had done it up right. I had them all fuming at me.

To make a long story short, Jeffrey didn't get to go, and we all stayed at home and tried to act normally. However, a black cloud hung over the entire day. Later, when Doug felt a bit better, we went to Perkins' for dinner and tried to have a good time. I can't remember what we ate, but I can remember it wasn't a happy meal together.

That afternoon, the Lord started to deal with me on the events of the day. I allowed God to speak to my heart, and to be truthful, I took the worst spiritual whipping that I ever care to have from my Heavenly Father.

As I listened, he said, "Randy, if you're ever going to win your kids, if you're ever going to see your kids make it to Heaven, you're going to have to change who you are, the way you do things, and your style of discipline. You're going to have to allow me to change who you are in order to become who I want you to be."

As fathers, there are times when we have to be very hard-nosed and unwavering. Equally, there are times when we just need to use a little common sense. You can't learn to be a father overnight. It takes experience. And trust me, when you try it, if you're honest, you'll mess it up, too. But if you're willing to work at it and stay pliable, you'll finally get it.

As I listened to the voice of God, I began to weep. In fact, I became so emotional that for the next two hours, I sat on the lounge chair and cried. I cried so much that I finally had Trish crying with me. I just couldn't quit crying.

It was very evident what I needed to do. Later that night, when the boys went to bed, it was time to face the music. I had to apologize to my son. The boys slept in bunk beds in the same room, and Jeffrey had the top one. As we got them situated for the night, I knew the moment was at hand.

Jeffrey was still feeling badly, and he knew I had been crying a lot that evening. As he lay there, I reached down and put my arms around him and said, "Jeffrey, I need to tell you that I'm sorry for the way that I treated you today. And I'm sorry for making the punishment so severe. I want to know if you'll forgive me."

By now, he was in tears as he reached up, put his arms around my neck and hugged me. I said, "Will you forgive your dad?" and he said, "Yeah."

As we embraced, I said, "Giz,"—a nickname he carries to this day— "I'm learning how to be a dad, and you're learning how to be a son. And if you'll help me to learn how to be a good dad, I'll try to teach you how to be a good son."

If you're not making a connection with your kids, maybe it's because you never use your reverse gear. I am thankful that over the years God has allowed me to understand the importance of using my reverse gear. Kids are forgiving, and they are tender. If you mess up, they're the first to know. And they're also the first to stand in line to receive the hug and a sincere apology when it's offered. Could it be that one of the reasons that we have lost so many of our young people is due to the fact that we often walk over top of them and never consider that we might need to ask them for forgiveness? It doesn't always have to be "our way or the highway."

Moms and dads: if you read this book and you don't get anything else out of it, please remember this point: Going back and saying you're sorry will get you more mileage in your relationship with your kids than any other thing you can do for them. They will respect you and love you for it.

I have learned that kids are like plants. They love attention, and the more you nurture them, feed them, and water them, the more they blossom and bloom. Even when I wasn't a Christian, there were a few times when I got the art of parenting right.

I always felt that the denomination of the church we attended while growing up, coupled with the generation of my parents, brought a fear of being able to openly discuss important matters like human sexuality, good touch/bad touch and how we should care for our bodies. Some things just weren't meant to be talked about, they said.

In my developmental years, I heard many things from neighborhood and school kids. I was just plain ignorant. I flat out didn't know what they were talking about. I was always looked down upon because I was the ignorant little boy who was always in the dark.

I remember hearing the kids talking about a male contraceptive device. I didn't have a clue what it was. The word I heard them using that day sounded to me like something you used to protect your dress shoes from the elements. I played along and acted like I knew what it was, but I didn't have a clue. Later that night, I finally got the nerve to ask my mom what it was, and she did her best to explain it to me. This happened when I was in the sixth or seventh grade. Man, I was so naïve.

Topics such as these were seldom talked about. However, if I asked a direct question, Mom did her best to answer. Dad rarely ever talked about these matters. He would only refer to the facts of life or the "birds and the bees." All I knew was that birds flew and bees stung. Hmm.

So, having been raised in this kind of environment where everything was hush-hush and we couldn't talk about anything of this nature, I decided that my kids were going to be educated—and not by the school system. They would be educated by Mom and Dad.

Many of the misunderstandings and misconceptions I carried about sexuality were because these things were never properly explained to me. Kids are naturally curious, and there's going to come a time when they're going to find out about such matters. They can either hear it explained by their parents the right way, or they can hear the story from Johnny and

Susie, their neighbors or school friends, which will most often be told from a warped perspective.

I am a naturally curious person. I love asking questions. I can't help it. If it's got moving parts, I have to know how it works and why. I also love finding out what people do, why they do it, and how it's done. If you lend me your ear, I'll ask you twenty questions. I've learned that the dumbest question is the one you don't ask.

When kids started talking in school, my curiosity got the best of me, and I had to find out more. Although the information was often inaccurate, it sure whetted my appetite, which led me on a path to pornography and misguided understandings about human sexuality. In later years, it contributed to my notion that women were only objects of my desire rather than people created by God who deserved equal respect.

I didn't want my kids to be caught up in that mess with the same misconceptions as I had. I vowed that before my kids ever went to school, they would have a basic understanding of who they were, the difference between good touches and bad touches, and have an understanding of where they came from and how they got here. Sex is a natural part of life, and we should not be afraid to discuss the issue with our kids.

Before the kids went to kindergarten, I took each of them on a 24-hour trip to Niagara Falls. Jeffrey was the first to go. Unfortunately at that time, there was a real upswing in child molestations across the country, and maybe that was why I was so determined to educate him.

Jeffrey was as naturally curious as I was about things. As we rode in the truck that day, I explained to him about his body and the natural use of his body. I told him he was about to enter into a new phase of his life when he started school. As a paramedic, I explained how God had made him. We talked about God giving him fingers, toes, hair, a nose, teeth and legs, and that the same God who gave him those parts also gave him his male anatomy. I explained to him that his male anatomy was used for two things, to excrete waste from his body and for reproduction at the proper time when he was married, but not until then.

"Nobody has the right to touch you in your private areas other than Mom and Dad but only if it's to help you in maintaining cleanliness, or a medical professional for medical reasons. Other than that, it's private. It's yours, a special gift from God." I also told him that if anyone at school, students or teachers, ever touched him in those areas for any reason, he needed to tell us immediately.

I told Jeffrey that when he started kindergarten, no doubt he would hear other kids use words like "sex" and four-letter words that would have the same meaning. I explained to him that sex was a natural part of the evolution of the stages of life.

During the course of this conversation, he began to ask me more questions: "How did I get here?" "How was I made?" This opened the door for me to explain that Mommy carried a microscopic seed within her called an egg, and that Daddy carried fertilizer called sperm, and that God had a made a place in Mommy for Daddy to deposit that fertilizer. The conversation was done innocently with no dirty connotations about it. I wanted him to know that it was natural and a gift from God.

It's amazing how God works. During our trip, we made a visit to Marineland on the Canadian side of the border where we saw two buffalo in the process of mating. And as you guessed, Jeffrey asked what they were doing. What a great opportunity.

"Remember when I told you about Daddy fertilizing the egg in that special place?" And it was like, "Oh, yeah." I said, "Well, that's what the daddy buffalo is doing to the mommy buffalo." End of question. I didn't go into detail, but gave him enough information to satisfy his curiosity.

Jeff did well. Not only did he understand, but he retained most of what I told him. When we got back home, Trish asked him what we had talked about and to my amazement, he repeated most of what we said word-for-word. It was obvious that he had a basic understanding. He went to school and never got caught up in the playground talk. I questioned him once about what kind of stuff that other kids were saying, and his reply was, "Oh, Dad, they're talking about stuff I already know."

A few years later, it was Doug's turn to go, and then when Lynn was old enough to use the restroom by herself, it was her turn. That was it. The curiosity had been taken out of it for all of them because they already knew about sex, and that it was natural and a gift from God. I'm thankful we gave them the right information early and in the proper context.

One thing I learned through this exercise was that each one of my kids was very different. When Doug went, he was not at the same level of maturity that Jeff was when he went, and therefore didn't require the same quantity of information as Jeff. With Lynn, not only did I take her to Niagara Falls, but Trish and I talked with her together. It's different with girls.

Regardless, when we were on the trip, we talked about anything they wanted to talk about. I talked openly with them because I wanted them to feel free to talk openly with me about any subject. They say there's a communication gap. I say it's a bunch of bunk. Communication happens when you talk to your kids. If you keep in contact with your kids and take a sincere interest in their lives, there will never be a gap in your communication.

From that point on, we did our best to explain things to them so that they would not be blindsided while transitioning into new phases of their lives. They would know beforehand that the emotions, physical changes, and feelings they were experiencing were absolutely normal and God-ordained.

In spite of the multitude of things I did wrong, there were a few bright spots in my early days of parenting.

CHAPTER 17

Shaken

The day I couldn't stop crying after trying to save a little boy's life was the beginning of the end of my career in emergency services.

As an EMS instructor, I well knew about critical incident stress breakdowns. In fact, I had lectured about it in many of my classes. I would often say, "It happens to everyone, and it will happen to you. It's not a matter of if, just a matter of when. And how you deal with it will affect the length of your career."

When it finally happened to me, the weight came crashing down in one sense worse than the chimney that had fallen on me years before.

By then, I was a Christian, and our ministry was growing. It was the end of the workday, and I was traveling home. A few minutes after leaving the station, driving east on Route 358 on the outskirts of Greenville, traffic began to back up. Up ahead, a man directed traffic near the entrance to a local mobile home park. On the opposite side of the road, a blue Caprice Classic faced west. It had sustained considerable damage to its hood and grill. I immediately thought the driver had hit a deer as they frequently cross the road in that area.

However, as I slowly passed by the scene, to my horror I saw a woman on the side of the road cradling a young child in her arms. The little boy appeared to be seven or eight years old. I couldn't believe my eyes. Somebody please pinch me. Was this a dream or reality?

When you're working a shift on the ambulance and the Plectron or pager goes off, the dispatcher will say something like, "Medic 41, respond

Code 3 to a motor vehicle accident with entrapment," and so on. As you race to the scene, you have time to think about what you might see. You mentally prepare for the worst. But the situation with this little boy was different. I was driving by, going home from work, with no time to adjust my thinking. My guard was down. I was vulnerable.

As a paramedic, I just couldn't drive by. That would have gone against my ingrained nature. To this day, it runs in my blood. If there's an emergency and I'm anywhere nearby, I'm in the thick of things. For example, in November 2011, while traveling on a bus tour to New York City, we came upon an accident that had happened probably just thirty seconds ahead of us. A truck rolled on its side down the median, and flames shot out of the engine compartment. The old paramedic nature kicked in. As the tour host on the bus, I immediately told the driver to pull over, and I was off the bus in seconds. I darted across the road, along with several other bystanders who were now on the scene, and together we rescued the driver from the burning truck. It's my nature.

I pulled to the side of the road near the mother and child, and flicked on my blue lights. In Pennsylvania, the law allows volunteers and EMS personnel to use blue emergency lights to assist them in navigating through traffic while responding to an incident.

The only medical equipment I had was the little first responder bag that I kept with me. So with that in hand, I left my vehicle and made my way across the road to the mother holding the little boy. I hollered to the guy directing traffic. "Has anyone called 911?" He said, "No." I hollered at him loudly again. *"Call 911!"*

As I hurried over, the mother screamed hysterically, "Can you help my baby, can you help my baby!"

I said, "Ma'am, I'm going to try to help your baby, but you're going to have to move away so I can work."

I saw what had happened. The little boy had been hit by the car. I knelt down and felt for a pulse and respirations. To my horror, there were none. He was in full cardiac and respiratory arrest, and I immediately began CPR. Using the pocket mask from my responder bag—a barrier between my mouth and his—I attempted to administer mouth-to-mouth and one-hand compressions rather than two, because he appeared to be pretty young.

While this was all happening, my world was in slow motion. I felt all alone, that whether this kid would live or die was in my hands, and I did not have the proper equipment with me to work on him.

Between the repetitions of CPR, I hollered at the man directing traffic, again asking if anyone had called 911. Again he said no. This time I screamed. *"Call 911! We need an ambulance!"*

The mother relentlessly shrieked in my ear, "Please help my baby! Please help my baby!" I fired back, "Ma'am, I'm trying to help your boy, but you're going to have to back off."

It seemed like an eternity. Finally, I heard a siren in the distance, a very welcome sound. By now, I was utterly frustrated. I couldn't get air into this kid's lungs to save his life. I had tried every trick in the book, everything I had been taught, and nothing would work. It was like blowing air against a block wall. Out of the corner of my eye, I saw flashing emergency lights, but it wasn't an ambulance. It was a Greenville/West Salem Township police cruiser.

I found out later that the Hempfield Police Department, in whose area we were, was tied up on another call and asked Greenville PD to respond in its place. When the officer got out of the cruiser, I recognized him, as we had been on many calls together. Officer John said, "Randy, what do you need?"

I said, "John, I need help. I can't get air into this kid. I cannot get air into his lungs. His airway is blocked. There's something going on."

Again, I tried every trick in the book—repositioning the airway, hyperextension, triple jaw-thrust maneuver. You name it, I tried it. I was a CPR instructor and an ACLS instructor and I couldn't get air into this kid? I was going nuts. I had trained the trainers. I had taught doctors and nurses all this stuff. I was at the top of the heap, and I was powerless to get air into this kid's lungs. I thought, "What am I doing wrong? *What am I doing wrong?*"

Officer John asked, "What do you want me to do first?" I said, "John, you've got to get this mother moved out of the way so I can work on the kid." He immediately took her by the shoulders and he stood her over by his cruiser. I saw him giving her a talking to, pointing his finger at her while he told her, "You're going to have to back off if you want us to be able to help your son." But I knew I would have acted the same way as she was, had it been my son.

Officer John came back over after he calmed mom down a little bit. I asked him to do compressions and I continued attempting mouth-to-mouth. Why didn't we have an ambulance here yet? What had seemed like an eternity to me probably was really only eight to ten minutes. It's amazing how roles reverse. Most often I would be the guy responding with the ambulance. Now I found myself on the other end, waiting on the ambulance. Not a good feeling.

Finally, Medic 41 and paramedic Will arrived on the scene. I said, "Will, this kid needs to be tubed right now. I can't get air into him. You've got to tube him right now." We secured the little boy to a backboard and did a load-and-go. Will's attempts to intubate him on the way were unsuccessful. Something drastic was obviously wrong.

When the ambulance left the scene, I stood in a sea of flashing emergency lights and personnel. I felt so alone. I'd been unable to help this little guy. I felt like a failure. I looked at the blue dress shirt I wore, and I could see the little boy's blood and gastric contents on my sleeves. I was a mess and felt dirty.

I remember asking one of my co-paramedics who had responded with Hempfield Fire Department for something to clean my hands with. As George was handing me the hand cleaner, he put his arm around my shoulder and asked if I was okay. He knew I was not dealing with the situation very well. Incidentally, George was one of the same paramedics who had responded to help me when the chimney fell on me some years earlier.

"George, I think I'm going to be okay. I'll be fine." He just patted my shoulder and he said, "All right."

I walked over to my van, got in and started the drive home. It felt like the floodgates opened up and I began to weep. I cried the whole way home. I could not understand it. I could not explain it. I couldn't quit crying.

My wife must have had the scanner on and heard that there had been an accident, and she knew that I had probably been there. When I walked in the door, I ripped off my shirt and commanded her, "Wash this!"

She said, "What's wrong?"

And I barked, *"Just wash it! Put it in the laundry right now!"*

I didn't want to talk about it. I sat in the lounge chair and continued to cry. I couldn't stop crying.

Before long, the phone rang. It was one of my co-supervisors, Pete. He said, "Randy, George told me you weren't doing too good. Are you all right?"

I said, "Pete, I'm feeling okay, but I can't quit crying. I just can't quit crying."

About another hour passed by and our general manager, Kent, called from where he lived in Ohio. "Randy, Peter told me you're not doing too well." I said, "Kent, I don't know what's going on. I just can't stop crying."

I cried most of that evening. I cried until I was just flat out of tears.

I think the thing that bothered me the most is that while I was working on the young boy, it seemed as though I was working on my own son, Jeffrey. He was nine at the time and almost the same size as the little boy I couldn't save.

The next evening, I found myself sitting alongside several other rescue personnel in a critical incident stress debriefing. To my surprise, I was not alone in my feelings. There were others who were handling this situation just about as well I was.

During the debriefing, we found out that the little boy had been walking with his mother in the big field not far from where he had been hit. He had been playing with a boomerang. He would throw it and it would come back to him.

Playfully, he threw his boomerang out across the road, and it came back. His mother told him, "Don't do that. You're going to get hit." But as kids often do, he ignored the warning, and he threw the boomerang one more time. Only this time, it didn't come back.

Instinctively, he raced across the busy, two-lane highway to retrieve his toy, and that's when it happened. The Caprice Classic caught him right in the neck at hood level. Apparently, in the last moment, he turned and gave a deer-in-the-headlights look. Upon impact, his entire trachea was fractured, along with his neck and upper chest area.

We found out at the debriefing that there was nothing any of us could have done differently, and there was no way any human was ever going to get air into him. He had been killed instantly.

After the debriefing, I understood it wasn't my fault. It wasn't because of something I had done wrong or anything else I could have done. It was the severe trauma that was the problem. Although I knew this, my confidence had been shaken, and I knew I wouldn't be able to handle many more incidents like that.

It wasn't generally my custom to view a body or meet the family of one of my patients who had passed away. But in the case of this little boy, I was compelled to go to calling hours at the funeral home and express my condolences to his parents. As I viewed his body, I saw that he had been highly traumatized, and things became more clear.

God also gave Trish and me an opportunity to minister to the needs of this family by giving them a gift certificate for groceries a few months later, and I was able to give his dad a ride home from work one night during a snowstorm.

After this, I continued on in EMS for a few more years. But it seemed as though there was a gradual pulling away, a phasing out of sorts, as I began accepting more administrative duties rather than run the risk of facing the unknown.

CHAPTER 18

Setting a New Course

During the course of my EMS career, I had my share of ups and downs with jobs. When I reflect, I see that from the time I accepted Christ, God was nudging me to a place where my family and I could become fully dependent on Him.

I knew God had a plan for our lives. However, it is only natural to need a crutch, and in my case, that crutch was my job. As long as I could maintain a good job, I didn't have to fully rely on God and could maintain a feeling of self-reliance.

As our ministry continued to grow, we had to spend a considerable amount of time maintaining and doing the behind-the-scenes chores that were associated with it. Ultimately, ministry work coupled with secular work took an inordinate amount of time which translated into a very hectic schedule.

Just when I would start to feel comfortable, God would nudge me again, getting us closer to the point when our only means of income would be generated from the ministry that He had called us to do.

The day final victory in my personal life came was the day I walked out of the office after thirteen and a half years of service with Gold Cross and Rural/Metro Ambulance Service. I went on to take the general manager's position at a medium-sized ambulance service located in Meadville. When I got the job, they were already in bankruptcy. Due to the fact that I had strengths in the area of marketing and public relations, I was hired to assist the owners with the task of generating new business, which would ultimately generate more income, in hopes of turning the company around.

In addition to being their general manager, I held the title of assistant chief and had anywhere from forty-five to sixty employees who were under my charge. This was a pretty heavy responsibility for a young man to handle.

When I left Rural Metro, I was making nearly $40,000 a year, plus benefits. When I took the new job in Meadville, I was making $42,000 plus a medical stipend. At first, everything seemed like it was falling into place, and life was grand.

The new job lasted only nine months. During the course of my employment, I found out why they were in bankruptcy. The owner of the company was spending money like a drunken sailor. In essence, he was stealing from himself. I'd leave work on a Friday only to return on Monday, and there would be massive amounts of money missing from the accounts that had money in them on Friday. It didn't matter—he took money out of payroll tax accounts. On one occasion, when I came back in on a Monday—which, by the way, was payday—$10,000 was missing from the payroll account. Talk about a nightmare. I eventually found out where the money had gone. He had bought a new boat.

While I was there, I hired a friend of mine to come in and help me with the accounting. In the month that he was there, he corrected more than 700 data entry errors in the system that was used for maintaining company accounts.

The day the $10,000 came up missing, I had no choice but to confront the owner and ask him what was going on. "How do you want us to cover payroll? There's not enough money in the accounts."

He had the audacity to say, "Go ahead and write the checks and give them out to the employees. The first ones who make it to the bank will win."

He was dead serious. There were times in the past, prior to my employment with the company, that this actually had happened. Employees would get their checks, only to get to the bank and hear the dreaded words, "Insufficient funds."

During the first week I was at the company, I held an employee meeting. I gave my word to all the employees that I would always be honest with them. When I confronted the owner, I insisted that we have an emergency employee meeting so that we could tell them it might be a few days before they could cash their paychecks. I was a Christian, and I told him, "I will not lie for you. I *will not* lie for you!"

Shortly after that, he reluctantly agreed, and we called an employee meeting to let them know that paychecks would be a few days late.

Later that afternoon, when I walked into the owner's office, he broke the news to me. "Randy, one of us has to go. It's either you or it's my wife and me—and it's not going to be us." My reply was, "Don't worry, by the end of today, you'll never know that I had been here."

At my request, they wrote me a check for two weeks' pay—which I cashed immediately. And that was that. I was out of a job.

On the way home, I could hear the words of my former boss saying to me when I left Rural/Metro, "You're crazy. You'll never find a situation as sweet as you have now." It's amazing how the devil will kick you when you're already down.

Not only could I hear those words that he said, but I could hear the words that I had so flippantly said when my former general manager asked me what I was going to do if the job in Meadville blew up in my face. "When I wake up the next morning, my wife will ask me if I want eggs. I will say yes; she will fix me those eggs, and life will go on."

As I continued driving home, I knew deep in my heart that I had made the right decision to leave Rural/Metro in order to move past the emotional and spiritual strain on my life as a result of the other woman. I accepted the job in Meadville because I thought I was honoring God. Yet here I was, nine months later, poof, up in smoke, crash and burn.

I'll never forget how I felt. I went home and got the ministry trailer and headed back for Meadville. A couple of guys helped me load all my stuff out of the office, and I was soon headed for home again. Man, it really hurt. Just when I thought we were doing fine, here I was without a job and without a plan. I didn't have a clue what I was going to do.

When I finally saw Trish and told her, she put her arms around me and cried. I said, "Honey, they can take away my job. They can take away everything I have. But they can't take away what's in my heart. And they can't take away my family."

I remember gathering the kids around the piano bench and putting my arms around them. I said, "Boys, Lynn, you're all I have. We're starting all over again."

I went through a period of depression, not understanding why this had happened. I kept questioning it. Losing a job like that is like going through a death. When you're the sole provider, you're the guy who's supposed to take care of your family. Then all of a sudden it's been stripped away from you through no fault of your own. And because you tried to do the right thing, the income for your family goes up in smoke.

Throughout my nine months of employment in Meadville, I had maintained contact with managers at Rural/Metro. It didn't take long before the news got back to them that I had been asked to leave. About two weeks after losing that job, I got a call from the general manager of EmergyCare Ambulance Service in Erie. "Randy, we're looking to put a new ambulance service in Meadville, and we understand that you just got let go. But we understand why you were let go and that it was not your fault."

He asked if I would be interested in helping them start the new service. This would give me an opportunity to compete with the company that had just let me go. I had the goods on them and knew their weaknesses. So I jumped at the chance. When my old company, Rural/Metro, found out what was happening, they offered to become a partner in this new service with EmergyCare. To make a long story short, I was brought on as their area manager, and a few months later, a brand new service began— Meadville EMS (MEMS).

The competition was fierce. I was a straight-up competitor and always maintained loyalty to the company I worked for. I would never do anything that was questionable but believed that we could grow our service by providing outstanding customer service. I knew this was going to be a tough fight.

When MEMS was born, we were the fourth service to be working in the Meadville region, too many ambulance services for that small an area. At the time, the national average for emergency calls was one call per day per ten thousand people. All four of our services were operating in an area of about 35,000 to 40,000 people. Sooner or later, one, two or three services would be out of business.

Everything went smoothly the first year. And then I started hearing rumblings that Rural/Metro was thinking about scaling back their operations in Pennsylvania. About the same time, I was hearing rumblings that EmergyCare might have to downsize because of the fierce competition they were facing from Mill Creek Paramedic Service.

For fourteen months, I was the one who had basically built this new service from the ground up. I had been involved from day one, from choosing the ambulances to designing the patch that we wore on our shoulders. This was my baby, and I loved it. Along with being area manager, I carried the title of Chief 41, and was again making $41,000 a year and full benefits. Life was good on both fronts. I had a good job, and the ministry was growing.

At the end of fourteen months, though, the operations manager of EmergyCare walked in and sat down in my office, and what he said was just like the San Francisco earthquake. It rocked my world and nearly killed me. "Randy, this is no reflection on you or anything you've done. Our board has been forced to make a financial decision, and we've had to let some of our managers go."

They eliminated four managerial positions that day, and one of the four was mine. They were top-heavy in management and they had to let some of us go. They replaced us with other mid-level managers with more seniority.

I kept saying, "What did I do? What did I do wrong?" He said, "It's nothing you did wrong. Just go home. Go home. The board's made a decision."

And just like that, it was stripped out of my hands. Poof! Gone with the wind.

Ironically, the day I was forced to leave was the very same day that Eastern Medical Ambulance Service and Lakeview Ambulance Service went out of business in Meadville. What a great way of saying thanks for a job well done. What began with four services was now down to two, MEMS and the other service that I used to work for.

Although they said it was no fault of mine, I still felt like a criminal. I was literally locked out of my office and allowed to take nothing with me. To this day, there are still some photos that were lost in the shuffle that I wish I had back. Later that week, they allowed me to go back in and retrieve most of my belongings in the presence of another manager. However, everything had been gone through. I knew they wouldn't find anything because I always ran a tight ship.

Talk about devastation. Twice in less than two years I had lost my job. As for my self-esteem, there was none. I was as low as a whale swimming at the bottom of the ocean. I don't think a snake could've crawled any lower. That's exactly how I felt.

Where was God in all of this mess? On the weekends, I was singing my heart out, doing my best to witness for the Lord and sharing our ministry with people all over. And now this? Believe you me, it's not hard to question God when you're going through something like this.

For the second time in less than two years, I got in the van and made the dreaded trip home. I was in tears as I called Trish, letting her know I had been let go. She couldn't understand it. She said, "What? What happened?"

When I got home and walked into the house, Trish put her arms around me and cried with me. Later that evening, I sat down on the piano bench and gathered Trish and the kids by my side and put my arms around all of them. I said, "Trish, they can take away my job. They can take away everything I have. But they can't take away what's in my heart. And they can't take away my family."

Once again, I was starting all over.

Regretfully, one more time, I slid into a state of depression. I vowed that I would never depend on any one company to provide my income. I remembered something my dad told me when I was younger. "Never put your eggs all in the same basket. It's better to be diversified and have eggs in lots of baskets. That way, if you lose one basket, you'll still have a lot of eggs in the other baskets." This would be my new motto in life. One thing about me—if I've given my word, I can stick to it until the cows come home.

EmergyCare gave me a severance package, $10,000 and four months of health benefits, and I was able to draw unemployment benefits at the same time. So in the short term, things would be okay.

About two weeks after losing the job, in my distress, I asked my pastor to take a trip with me to Dobbins Landing on the bay front in Erie, Pennsylvania. Being near the water at Dobbins Landing was always a place of refuge, and I would often find my way there for times of reflection and meditation. However, this day was different. It was the end of an era. I took my gold chief's badge from my uniform and skipped it as far as I could into the bay. The chapter of EMS was over.

To help occupy my time, I used some of the severance money to buy a little Jeep with a six-foot snowplow on it, and decided to get into the snow plowing business to make a little cash on the side. Within the first couple weeks of advertising that I was available, I had more jobs than I knew what to do with. I was plowing churches, businesses and residential driveways.

Talk about a blessing! A local contractor called and asked if I would go to Meadville and plow snow for a commercial lot that he had to keep clean. One week, the snow was relentless, but I was loving it! I had contracted with him for thirty dollars an hour. I pushed more snow that week than I care to remember. I kept pushing it into big piles and they came in with high-lifts and put it into dump trucks and hauled it away.

It's amazing what you can do when you set your mind to it. My dad always told me that I was a little bit like my Uncle Gary who was enterprising and seemed to find many creative ways to make a buck. I guess it runs in my bloodlines. That winter, I prayed for snow, and we were blessed with an abundance. Every time I checked my wallet, there was always money there for the extra things that we needed.

When not traveling with the ministry or plowing snow, I was sitting at home doing a good job of getting into Trish's hair. Quite honestly, I was driving her nuts. There were days that I was so depressed that I just about had her out of her mind. I remember her saying, "Randy, do something! Go pump gas if you have to. Do *something*. Just don't sit there and sulk all day. The least you could do is to get the newspaper and go through it to see what kinds of jobs are available."

I took her advice and started checking for ads. I remember seeing one for motor coach operators which sounded interesting. I loved traveling with our ministry, and I loved traveling in general. This might be right down my alley. So I applied to go to driving school.

When I went for my first interview, they handed me a map of Pennsylvania and asked me to find a little town that I didn't even know existed—Trout Run, Pennsylvania. Maps were no problem for me at all. I loved reading them, and as a child often spent many hours looking at the road atlas and dreaming of traveling to faraway places. I knew how to navigate my way on a road map. After easily finding Trout Run, they asked me to put the map away. They were checking to see if I knew how to fold a map. No problem there.

Driving school was great. You went to school for four hours a day, four days a week, Monday through Thursday, for six weeks, with no pay. At the end of six weeks, if you had successfully learned how to drive a five-speed, a seven-speed and a forty-five-foot Prevost motor coach, you *might* be able to get hired on. Sounds like a "great" deal. But by now, I was starting to get used to living on the edge and decided it was worth a try.

Driving school was tough. Some of the instructors were like drill sergeants, and there were some days I felt like I was in boot camp. They messed with you, played with your mind, trying to see if they could get you to break mentally.

I'll never forget the day we were on a training run. My instructor sat down on the passenger side of the motor coach. I had already done my pre-trip inspection of the bus and was sitting in the driver's seat, ready to go. I asked, "Where are we heading?" His response: "Don't worry where we're heading. Just follow the bus in front of you and don't lose him." I wanted to turn right around and smack him right there. But seeing how that would not be the Christian thing to do and would eliminate any possibility of getting hired, I decided to do what he told me to do.

When we finally got to Austinburg, Ohio—which, by the way, was where we were going—another driver instructor who was on the bus following me came up and thrust his finger under my nose. He was a short, pudgy little guy, about as wide as he was tall. He ranted, "You *never* leave the bus behind you!" I was so intent on following the bus ahead of me that I had smoked the guy behind me, left him in the dust. He was really giving it to me, cleaning my clock.

When I finally had a chance to speak, I said, "You don't understand. My instructor didn't tell me where we were going, other than I was to follow the bus ahead of me and not lose him." When he heard this, he verified what I had said with the instructor on my bus. Then they both laughed like idiots! They were just messing with me. When you're traveling down the road driving a forty-five-foot motor coach with fifty-six people aboard, you'd better be able to keep your cool and hold it together.

After graduation, I was offered a part-time position as motor coach operator. A few weeks later, I started to drive for various tour companies who chartered buses from the company I worked for.

I was there a total three and a half years. About a year and a half into it, I was on a run down to Pittsburgh International Airport to pick up passengers. Just before crossing Neville Island on I-79 south, I was traveling through a construction zone and a semi-truck slammed his brakes on in front of me. There was considerable glare from the sun on the windshield that day, which may have prevented me from seeing his brake lights. To this day, I'm not sure if his lights were even working. Regardless, it was still my fault. I had been following too closely. I rear-ended the back of his tractor-trailer dump truck.

When I hit him, the front of the bus caved in all around me. I literally stood on the brake pedal so hard that I bent it in half. I still have the brake pedal from that bus in my basement.

When you're driving in the front of a motor coach and you have an accident, you're a sitting duck. There's not much in front of you to absorb the impact. When the bus finally came to a stop, I set the emergency air brakes and started to untangle my right leg from underneath the crumpled dashboard. By now, my right foot was stinging with pain, and when I finally got out of the bus, I was definitely limping.

After a quick trip to the hospital for X-rays, they determined that I had broken two toes on my right foot. But other than my wounded pride, I would live.

Although it was ultimately my fault, the company decided to keep me on rather than let me go, due to the fact that there were extenuating circumstances. After that, I continued working part-time with the company to the point where I was making about $19,000 a year. It was great having the extra income to help with our ministry. Once again, I felt like God was blessing. However, in order to make that $19,000, I had to spend a lot of time on the road and away from the family.

One morning I received a call from the dispatcher to run the airport shuttle between Erie and Cleveland. This call came at a very stressful time, when I was worried about several things and attempting to replace some of our sound equipment. I should have turned down the trip. One thing I should mention about the company I worked for, if you refused a trip, they would make sure it would be a while before they called you again. So you quickly learned to accept just about anything they threw at you. Otherwise, it might be two weeks before you worked again.

Later that afternoon, I started my shift. I drove the bus from Greenville to Cleveland, picked up my passengers and headed for Erie, only to turn around to go back to Cleveland to do it all again. This was going to be a long night and I was already running on little sleep, as I had spent a lot of time working on ministry items that week. When I got back to Erie from my last run, twelve or thirteen hours later, I parked the bus and then took the old van that was sitting there back to Greenville.

On the way home, I was exhausted. About 3:30 a.m., I called the garage and asked the mechanic if the vehicle I was driving had to go back out the next morning. I told him I was really tired and wanted to go to my home (which was located along the route I was traveling to the garage), and sleep for a couple of hours before taking the van back to the garage later in the morning. His answer was, "Nope, you can't do that. The van you're driving is scheduled to go out around 7:00 in the morning."

Now get this—they probably had five or six other vans sitting on the lot that could have gone out in the morning. But for whatever reason, he insisted that the van I was driving was the one that had to go out.

I said, "All right, I'll try to make it," and I almost did. Less than a half-mile from the garage, coming into Greenville, I fell asleep at the wheel. I don't know to this day how I'm still alive to tell this, other than it being the hand of God.

At one place, the road curves to the right, but I kept heading straight, straight for the side of a house. When I started off the road, I hit a road sign—a Yield or No Passing zone sign or something like that—and that woke me up. I jerked the wheel to the right and by doing so, avoided slamming into the side of the house. But in the process, I cleaned out several other signs that were in a cluster along the side of the road. Had I hit one that slapped the windshield at a different angle, it could have come in sideways and severed my head from my body.

When I finally got the van under control, I could see the parking lot of the bus garage just ahead. In addition to missing the house, I just barely missed hitting a car parked underneath a carport alongside it. To this day, other than the hand of God, I don't know how I avoided it. But the van was demolished.

I had made the statement after the first crash with the bus that if I was ever involved in an accident again, I would resign immediately. I told the manager I would and he said, "You may not want to do that right away. They may not want to let you go because you did call in and tell them that you might not make it, but they insisted you bring the vehicle back."

Well I knew it was inevitable that they were going to let me go, and they did. And one more time, something that I thought I could depend on, a little bit of extra income coming into our family and ministry had been stripped away.

Once again, God protected me, but I finally got the message loud and clear that He'd been trying to get through my thick head for a long time. I needed to be fully reliant on Him, rather than always needing a crutch, the extra income from a job.

Since then, I went on to get my Class A commercial driver's license. And here and there, and every now and again, I drove motor coaches or dump trucks or a tractor/trailer for various companies, but nothing regular. In fact, it has been close to three years since I have worked anywhere other than in ministry. My priorities and my focus have changed.

On the days that I do work for someone else, I refer to them as vacation days, because it gives me a break from the day-to-day routine of managing the ministry and the responsibilities of pastoring a church. And somehow, I have even managed to learn to say no when I am busy and stressed out.

An added blessing of the ministry was that while I was driving motorcoaches, I realized I had the knack of coordinating and booking tours. A small company that we own and operate from our house called Christian Fellowship Tours began then and continues to this day. The people who travel with us are mostly the fans and friends of our ministry, some 4,000 families who are on our mailing list. At our peak, we were doing approximately twenty-five trips a year. Now that I am pastoring full time and in the process of downsizing in other areas, we have dropped to about eight trips per year. And God continues to bless.

Everything I did in the flesh to make sure our family had financial stability was always stripped away, and from the time of my last accident until now, our ministry has been a faith one, depending on God to provide for our needs so we can remain focused on the tasks that He has called us to do. And He has never let us down.

One of the hardest things for God to get through my thick head was that He did not want me to have a crutch to lean on because it is my tendency to rely on that crutch rather than Him. It's hard to let go of a personal safety net. As a father and as a husband, I have been given the responsibility of providing for my family, and it was difficult to let go of the crutch of self-reliance and become fully dependent on God.

What God wanted me to understand is that *He* is our safety net. *He* is our crutch. And just like the old hymn, "Leaning on the Everlasting Arms," I had to learn to lean on the Master. I had been so bull-headed and stubborn. Unfortunately, it took all those crazy hard knocks for me to understand that God wanted me to devote my attention to His work rather than following my own desires.

People often ask me if I ever formally went to college, and I remind them that I carry a Ph.D. from HKU—Hard Knocks University, graduating at the top of the class.

CHAPTER 19

The Van's Possessed

I f I ever have doubts as to whether our ministry was ordained of God, all I have to do is look back at all the doors God has opened, the many miracles performed, and how He has provided for our every need. When I reflect, my doubts quickly vanish.

When I was saved, we were $30,000 in debt, mostly because of my lifestyle. I was never happy, never satisfied and was always looking for something, a tangible item or a new thrill that would hopefully provide a sense of contentment. At one point, over the span of about a year and a half, I traded vehicles five times. With each trade, I bought a new vehicle, which only created more problems. The balance of the previously owned vehicle was always tacked onto the loan of the newly purchased vehicle. Not a good thing.

Then there was the credit card debt. If I saw something I wanted, I bought it. When you're not a Christian, your entire concept of managing money is often distorted, as was the case with me. When it came to financial matters and money management, I had no sense of direction.

Needless to say, when I got saved, we were in pretty sad financial shape, trying to reestablish our home, pay all the bills, keep food on the table, and face an overwhelming mountain of debt. Add in the absurdity that God called me to start a music ministry, so now we would have to spend even more money.

It had been so easy to dig myself into this hole, but I was going to need a dredge to dig myself out. Filing bankruptcy was not an option. I would have to tackle this situation in order to learn my lesson, and with a little bit of self-discipline, ingenuity, and a lot of hard work, we could make it.

Times were tough and funds were low, often nonexistent. But each and every time, miraculously, every need was met.

One time, we were so low that there was no money available to spend for basic necessities like bread, milk and eggs. We were trying to buy groceries on a biweekly basis; however, with three kids, we often ran out of the essentials.

One day Trish said, "Honey, when you go to the post office today, we need a miracle."

When I arrived at the post office, would you believe it, there was a check in the mail from AT&T for $75. We could cash that check if we agreed to switch our service from MCI. Well, it didn't take a rocket scientist to figure out what we did. That $75 check was like a thousand dollars to us. We made phone calls, switched back to AT&T, and went and got groceries. God is so good.

Then there was the time when, after recording my first Christmas album *Down from His Glory*, a preacher friend of mine asked me if he could have five cassettes to sell at his church. I gave him the cassettes, and he told me that as soon as he got paid for them, he would send me the money. Two years passed, and I never heard another thing from him, let alone saw any payment. We used to sell the cassettes for $10 apiece, so he owed me $50. We figured we'd never hear from him again. In fact, by this time, he wasn't even in the ministry any longer.

I'll never forget the beautiful, sunny day when Trish came to me again and said, "Randy, we need a miracle today. We need milk, bread, and eggs, and I'm totally out of money." By now I was really feeling the pressure. I couldn't work anymore than I already was working. In fact, it felt like I was working day and night. On top of working, we were playing concerts on weekends, but the offerings just weren't that great. One could say right then and there that I had every reason to throw my hands up and quit. The Bible says that a man who doesn't provide for his family is worse than an infidel, and here I was, a new Christian, and I couldn't even provide basic essentials for my family.

Shortly after Trish and I had the conversation, I went to the post office, and unbelievably, there was a check in the mail from this former preacher for $50 along with a letter of apology. My feelings were indescribable. You would have thought I had just struck it rich. I learned a lesson that day—God's timing is amazing. He's on time, every time, just in time.

Then there was the time I was asked to sing for a wedding, and on the way to rehearsal, I hit a thirteen-point buck with the van we used for ministry, our 1993 Ford Aerostar. This was the van that we'd purchased in an attempt to consolidate our bills and to downsize into one vehicle. It was our main vehicle, used for everything. Our monthly payments were tremendous and required a large portion of our monthly budget.

And now, traveling on a dark road late in the evening, I hit this deer head-on and pulverized the whole front end of that van. In retrospect, the van should have been demolished. However, estimates came in that it could be fixed for $5,000. We didn't have any choice. We had to get it repaired.

By the way, the deer—it was huge, the biggest buck I'd ever seen. The Pennsylvania Game Commission called the deer atypical, as the antler points were all webbed together. We got to keep the deer and had him for several meals.

But on top of all our other financial troubles, this was the last thing we needed to have happen to us. I've always heard that the Lord will test you. Well, let me tell you, this van was now the major source of frustration in my life. There were days when I wanted to push it over a cliff and forget I ever owned it.

The mechanics said they fixed the van. However, it had sustained so much damage that they couldn't get everything to line up right in the engine. Therefore, we went through five water pumps, four radiators, a heater core, two clutch fan assemblies and three engines before we finally got it to run right.

I was driving up Route 18 just north of Greenville one day, and the whole fan assembly went flying off into the radiator. It was amazing. You would have thought this van was possessed! It was just crazy. This van caused me to buy a membership with AAA just for towing services. We'd go to a concert and overheat. We'd get it fixed again, and then we'd have an engine blow, and I was off to the junkyard for a used engine.

In spite of our frustrations with the van, our ministry continued to grow, and God continued to bless. There were a few times at concerts when people were compelled to walk up and give us a "green handshake." That's when someone comes and shakes your hand and there's a ten- or twenty-dollar bill left in your palm. And then there were the times when someone walked up and said he felt led to support our ministry and tucked a folded check into my shirt pocket for $500. Wow, talk about a booster shot in the arm! We sure did thank the Lord for the faithfulness of His people.

The neat thing about this story is that every night when we would pray with the kids, Doug would say these words at the end of his regular bedtime prayers: "Dear Jesus, please help Mom and Dad get enough money to pay off the van." When he said this, he was sincere. Somehow, our little boy could understand the problems we were facing with this van, and his faith was childlike.

As Paul Harvey would say, here's the rest of the story:

I had just had the vehicle repaired for the umpteenth time. At this time I was working at Meadville Area Ambulance Service. It was Friday afternoon, and we were scheduled to be in Keyser, West Virginia, for a concert on Sunday morning. I had to make a run out to Conneaut Lake, Pennsylvania, to visit a mutual aid ambulance service. As I was traveling up the big hill on Route 322 out of Meadville, I heard the van making a crazy clicking noise, just *click-click-click*. And all of a sudden it started to shut off.

I pulled into the Burger King at the top of the hill because I'd planned to stop there and get lunch on the way. I ordered it to go, started the van and headed for Conneaut Lake. About another mile down the road, it happened again. The clicking noise turned into a *da-runk, da-runk, da-runk, grrromp.* And engine number two gave up the ghost.

Fortunately, I was able to coast into a parking lot and called our paramedic supervisor who also was a mechanic. I asked him if he would come take a look at the van. He came out, looked at the engine and said, "Yep, I think you just blew the engine."

I said, "You gotta be kidding me." So I got on the cell phone and said, "Trish, you're never going to believe this, but we just blew the engine up in the van again."

She said, "Aw, honey." What else could she say?

I had this huge debt on me, and I was thinking, "Lord, what? Why? I'm trying to sing for You. I'm trying to minister for *You*. And everything is going crazy."

I knew we were booked for a rally day concert in Keyser, West Virginia on the weekend. And the following weekend, we were supposed to sing in Tunkhannock, Pennsylvania, up near Scranton in northeast Pennsylvania.

I didn't know what to do other than get a brand new engine. So I told Trish, "All right, get on the phone and call around to the different garages and see where we can buy a short-block three-liter V6 engine to put in this van for the cheapest price."

Trish called around and wouldn't you know, the garage that had the short-block engine at the cheapest price, including installation—for $2,500—was in Conneaut Lake, the direction I was headed. So once again, I called AAA and had the van towed out there.

We had been saving every penny we could in order to pay this van off, and by now we had saved $3,000 to $3,500. We had been praying and asking God to help us get out from under the huge debt load that we had inherited from a previous life full of bad financial decisions. Just when we thought we were getting ahead, now here we were, back to square one.

I asked the guys at the garage if they could have the van ready for us for the following weekend, and they said no problem. However, we still needed a set of wheels to get us to the concert in West Virginia. I called our pastor and asked if I could borrow his van. It was an old panel van with seats bolted into it. It was a rattletrap vehicle and very beat up. But what else could we do but hook it up to our trailer and set off for West Virginia?

That Sunday morning, at the end of the service, we were loading up the trailer before dinner, and my wife came over and said, "Honey, you're never going to believe this."

I said, "What?"

She said, "The preacher's van, the one that we borrowed, is leaking antifreeze all over the place."

I was nuts and just about out of my mind. When I looked under the van, she was right. There was a huge puddle of antifreeze. "Lord, what are you doing to me? What are you trying to do to me?" By this time, I was nearly beside myself with frustration.

The pastor of the church in West Virginia said, "This is definitely an ox-in-the-ditch situation." He knew a guy who might be able to look at the van for us. So we unhooked the trailer and took the van down to a little garage that was across from the church. The guy there looked at it and said, "I think it's just a leak in the radiator." He put a tube of sealant in it and said, "We're going to let it run for a little bit and see if the leak will clear up."

We went back to the pastor's house. Over dinner we talked about how we'd just take it easy going home and maybe we could make it.

It's a totally helpless feeling when things seem out of your control. You're trying to minister for the Lord and proclaim His Word in your music, and while you're doing this, you feel like you're getting bombarded from every angle. Shamefully, I must admit that I was not in the best of spirits. I was pretty down, and it wouldn't have taken much persuasion for me to quit.

As we sat at the dinner table, the pastor's phone rang, and to my surprise, it was for me. In my mind, I groaned. "Well, I wonder what else has happened."

On the phone was a man from our local church in Meadville. "Randy, we heard about your van situation, and there were several of us this morning who just felt led to take up a love offering for The Keelings. Would you like to know how much came in the offering?"

I said, "Brother, I don't even know what to say. At this point in time, I'll take any good news I can get. I'd love to know how much it was."

He said, "We received around $1,795 in the offering, and we're going to put it toward the new engine for your van. We're going to make the check payable to the dealership, and you can pay the balance on your own."

I didn't know what to say. Talk about a lift of your spirits. Our God is so amazing. Just when I was feeling like quitting, my Heavenly Father was lifting me up again. "Thank you, thank you," I said. "Praise God! *Praise God!*"

In addition to telling us about the offering, he also told us that if we got into a jam on the way home, he would come with his truck and help us get our trailer home.

As we traveled home, Trish and I were rejoicing because we thought God had really done an amazing thing. But the best was yet to come.

The following Saturday, we made it to Tunkhannock with our van and the newly installed engine, paid for mostly by a love offering from the church. Everything seemed to be clicking along fine now. We had great concerts that weekend, and it seemed as though we had weathered the storm of the possessed van.

The following Wednesday night after coming home from Tunkhannock, we were at prayer meeting. On the way out the door, unbeknownst to me, a little old lady handed my wife an envelope. She told Trish, "You're not allowed to tell anyone about this or where it came from. This is a gift from God." She stressed, "It's a gift from God, and you're not allowed to open it until you get home."

When we got home from prayer meeting, Trish went back into the bathroom and opened the envelope and immediately called for me. It was amazing. I don't have the words to describe my feelings. Inside that envelope was a check made payable to our family in the amount of $3,000!

I looked at it and was immediately shouting happy. I was now in the kitchen hollering and praising God, and called for the kids to come. When they all gathered around me, I showed the check to them, covering up the name. "Boys, don't ever, ever think that God doesn't answer prayer. Look at this, look at this right here. *Right here.*" Then we gathered together as a family and sang the Doxology, with the words, "Praise God from whom all blessings flow."

I called my dad on the phone and I said, "Dad, you're never going to believe this. Tomorrow, we're going to pay off the van." He was stunned.

Then I called my friend Rick. He knew we had been struggling. When he found out the good news, he had a shouting spell over the phone. He yelled, *"Praise God! Hallelujah!"* He knew what kind of frustrations we had been going through.

Finally, almost four years to the day after our first concert, we were getting out from under the load of debt that had been on our shoulders.

The check came on Wednesday night and on Thursday morning I walked into the bank and I told the teller, "I'm here to pay off the van." With the $3,000 from the check and the $1,795 that came in the love offering, coupled with some savings that we still had, not only did we pay off the van, but we had a new engine and there was a little bit left in savings. Our God is an awesome God.

The teller looked at me and said, "It must make you feel really good." I said, "Ma'am, you don't even have a clue. This isn't even my money. This is God's money. He's the one helping us pay this off."

This incident put an unbelievable faith in me. From then on, there was never a doubt that God would supply our every need.

CHAPTER 20

Miracles

Another financial miracle happened just two weeks before my second accident with the bus company. We were in concert at a church just outside of Greenville. That night after the concert, a man and his wife, an older couple, hung around the back. It appeared that they were waiting until we finished loading our equipment so they could talk to us. I remember commenting to Trish, "This is kind of strange." In fact, we heard them tell the pastor, "Don't worry. We'll stay and lock up the church."

After we finished loading our equipment, we were just about ready to say our final goodbyes to this couple and they said, "There's a reason we stuck around late. We want to talk to you."

They gathered our family around in a circle and the man began to speak. He said, "My mother passed away recently and my brother and I had to split up the estate. Now that all the bills are paid, we have both taken our portion of the inheritance.

"As I have been praying, God has laid it on my heart that we need to support the ministry of The Keelings. An amount kept coming to my mind, but I didn't know how my wife would react. So I began to pray that God would lay the same amount on her heart.

"One morning at breakfast, she spoke up and said, 'I've been thinking, maybe we need to take some of that money you received from your mother's estate and support The Keelings.' He said, 'I've been thinking the same thing. I've been praying that the Lord would lay it on your heart to do this as well. Honey, how much were you thinking?' She gave the figure and he said, 'That's exactly the amount I've been praying about, and I've been feeling the same way.'"

That night, each one of the kids received a check for $500, and Trish and I received a check for $3,500. *Wow. What a blessing.* We thanked them profusely. We hardly knew what to say, we were so overwhelmed.

Surprisingly, this blessing came at a time when we seemed to be doing okay financially. In fact, I remember Trish asking, "What are we going to do with the money?"

I really didn't have an answer for her. I said, "Well, we'll just put it in the bank and keep it there."

They say for every mountaintop experience, there's usually a valley not far behind. I can remember praying, "God, don't make the valley too hard," because I suspected that something was coming. Sometimes the devil can really fight you on things like this.

Two weeks after receiving this blessing, it was very clear why the money had been given. I had the accident in the van while driving home from Erie for the bus company and was terminated.

Looking back, God had it all under control. I never really made much money driving a bus, but it was just enough to fill in the holes. Needless to say, the $3,500 filled in the holes and kept us going for the rest of the year. Even when we didn't know it, God was looking out for us, making sure that all of our needs were supplied.

You'll get tired of me saying this, but our God is an awesome God! Each time an incident like this happened, I learned to trust Him more and more, and my faith continued to grow stronger. By now, I knew my God could do *anything*.

With each job loss and/or accident that happened, I was forced to trust Him more, to learn to fully rely on our Heavenly Father. I love the little song that says he owns the cattle on a thousand hills and the wealth in every mine. My friend Jesse Arnett says God owns all the taters in the hills as well. Each blessing bolstered me to get more involved in ministry, to go all out for Him as hard as I could go, to work harder to make a greater impact on more lives.

For several years, our ministry was the sole source of income for our family. Along the way, there were a few bumps, but every time, God was there to smooth them right out. We weren't getting rich, but we were getting the bills paid. And we were able to pay a weekly stipend to the kids for all their hard work. They were really putting their hearts into it.

In addition to all that, we were able to keep on schedule with our recording needs. Our first major family recording was *Changed*. We were able to contract with Roger Tally as our arranger and producer. Now we had some of the best names in the business working for us. My wife often wondered and worried, "Randy, where's it going to come from?" Once again, God moved on the hearts of people.

Without making a public plea, checks started to arrive in the mail. The amounts varied—$15, $50, $75, $100 and $500. Some were consistent every month, but many weren't. But when it was all done, we always had enough to pay all the bills.

From where I stand, I clearly see that God works through people who would be the last you would ever think to support your ministry. And the amazing thing is they came from all denominations—Baptists, United Brethren, Nazarene, Presbyterian, you name the flavor. It's so easy for us to stereotype and judge people because of their denomination and affiliation. But as the song says, it's not what's over the door, it's what's in your heart. And I'm reminded that God looks on the inward man rather than the outside.

One thing I have come to learn—there are a lot of people who may not look like conservative holiness people, but they are still a part of God's family. In the beginning part of our music ministry, I attempted to cater mostly to the conservative holiness churches and found that all I was doing was trying to live up to a standard created by man so we could get bookings.

I was hungry to get booked at some of their largest churches and camp meetings, but there was always something standing in the way. And it seemed like the goal line was always being moved. Sort of like a carrot dangled in front of you—you can see it, you can smell it, but it's purposely kept just a fraction of an inch out of your grasp. We were never going to be able to live up to their expectations or their ever-changing standards. There would always be a reason why we would be rejected.

Our kids played in band in a public school. That was a negative. Stories were going around that I was trying to separate the couple who sang with us by standing in between them. I was really just trying to hear the parts so we could harmonize! The ties I wore were too bright or too wide. Once, when I was looking for a church to attend, the pastor couldn't even look me in the eye, but made sure to look at the color of my tie. We never attended his church again. Some people even accused my wife of running out on the stage and acting like "Hollywood." I still laugh profusely about that today. That is so not her. If you met my wife, she is as timid as a meek little lamb.

One man at a camp meeting had the audacity to poke his finger into my chest and say, "What are you doing with all the money you're making?" I was trying to remain a Christian as I replied, "Frankly, it's none of your business." What he didn't know was that I was broke.

One day while praying, God clearly revealed to me that those who were healthy were not in need of a physician, but those who were sick needed the physician. And again I heard that gentle voice saying, "Randy, I have not called you to a particular denomination for just a few people. I have called you to reach out to the world, and that means all people."

It was kind of my Apostle Peter experience when he had his vision of the unclean animals coming down in the sheet and the words of Jesus saying, "Do not call something unclean if God has made it clean." After that experience, a whole new world opened up to us. We were now singing in just about any and every denomination you could think of, and God was blessing us even more.

Another great blessing happened while I was driving a bus for Cooley Coach and Charter to Charleston, West Virginia, for a Promise Keepers rally. My wife called me at the hotel and asked if I remembered a guy I had met by the name of Loren.

She said, "He remembered meeting you a couple of years ago while you were driving on a bus trip in Lancaster, Pennsylvania."

I remembered having a conversation with Loren. He owned a very large farming operation in Ashtabula County, Ohio, raising dairy cattle and crops. I'd mentioned, "If you ever decide you want to sell some beef, let me know. I'd love to buy some from you."

He said, "Okay, I'll keep that in mind."

Two years had passed since I talked with Loren, and now Trish said I needed to contact him. Incidentally, we were scheduled to sing at his church in Pierpont, Ohio, the next Sunday morning. I called him on

Saturday and said, "Loren? This is Randy Keeling." He said, "Oh, yeah, how are you doing?"

We exchanged pleasantries and finally he said, "The reason I wanted you to call, do you remember when you asked if I had any beef for sale?"

"Yeah," I replied.

"Do you have any room in your freezer?"

I said, "Yes." But all we had was a little, teeny chest freezer in our kitchen.

Loren said, "That's great. I'll tell you what, you guys are coming to my church tomorrow, and I have a half a beef for you at no charge."

I said, "Loren, no, I gotta pay you something for it. We gotta give you something." He said, "No, God has laid it on my heart, and has told me that I'm supposed to give it to you as my way of helping your ministry and your family." I asked him if we could help pay the cost of cutting and wrapping, and he said there would be no charge for that, either.

You could have knocked me over with a feather. I didn't even know what to say.

He said, "You just keep doing what you're doing. Just keep ministering. That's what you've got to keep doing. Now tomorrow after church, I want you to come over to my house. I want to give you a tour of the farm."

That next Sunday afternoon, we got our tour, and it was great. Before we left, he said, "Oh, by the way, when I talked to you on the phone yesterday, Randy, I was wrong. This isn't half a beef. It's a whole beef."

"You've gotta be kidding me." We had to go to Lowe's the next day to buy a 15-cubic-foot freezer which I own to this day.

From that time until the present, God has continued to bless our family and our table with an abundance of beef that He has provided through the hands of Loren and Nancy Ring, our dear friends from Monroe Township, Ohio. By now, we have been blessed so many times that I have lost count of the number of phone calls we have had from them, and the number of whole beefs he has provided to our family. Since meeting them, there have been very few times that Trish has had to purchase beef. When the freezer is about empty, miraculously, he calls again. When you think about it, it's overwhelming. When we offer to pay, he says, "You just keep doing what you're doing."

Loren and Nancy are two of the finest people you will ever meet. They have become great friends, and we love them dearly. Every time I eat a hamburger or a steak, I'm thanking God for a man like Loren who has kept our table full. When we go out for dinner and eat a steak, it's very easy to tell that it didn't come from Loren's farm. His beef is far superior, and we're spoiled.

Over the years, God has brought many wonderful people into my life. Another one is a guy named Steve. I call him Pops, and he calls me his fourth son. Together, he and I have stormed the gates a few times, laughed like crazy, and created many lasting memories. Whenever I need someone to talk to, I usually call Steve. He's in his mid-70s, sort of a cross between the big brother you never had and the dad you always wanted. Let me tell you a little bit about him.

I'll never forget the day he came to help me work on an addition to the house. We were using a .22-caliber nail gun, and it decided it didn't want to fire. In our attempts to fix it, he pressed the end of the nail gun down on the small set of wooden steps originally attached to our home, but which now sat out of the way in the yard. After repeatedly pressing on the barrel and yanking the trigger, the nail gun fired straight through the wooden deck, knocking off a fairly large triangular piece. I whirled around in time to see Steve going head over tin kettles toward the ground. My first thought was, "Oh, my goodness, I killed him!"

Well, we both survived and laugh about it often.

Then there was the time he was helping me fell a large cherry tree in the backyard. The tree was close to the house, and we needed to make sure we dropped it in the right direction.

The tree split into a fork. One part had successfully been felled, and we were attempting to fell the second part. I chained a small Cub Cadet tractor to the tree, and while I cut, Steve pulled. The tree started to twist toward the backside of the house. We immediately stopped our activity and I hollered at Steve, "I'm going to get the Jeep so we can hook on and pull a little harder in the right direction."

As I ran for the Jeep, I set my brand new Husqvarna 455 Rancher—a *man's* chain saw—on the stump of a nearby tree. After securing the Jeep to the chain, we cut just a little bit more on the tree and then I began to pull with the Jeep. The tree toppled to the ground and we missed the house.

Steve said, "I smell gasoline." My heart sank. The new chain saw, which had been sitting on the old stump, had been in the direct line of fire of the falling tree and was now in a thousand pieces. Pieces and parts went in every direction. I wanted to bawl.

When Steve and I think of that incident today though, we laugh like hyenas—now.

Several days while I was driving semi-trucks, I invited Steve to ride along. Steve had been a trucker for years, and at one time owned his own rig. One day, I was driving an old Peterbilt. We were in the yard unloading bark scrappings. As the conveyor on the truck ran, Steve and I were outside the truck making sure that everything was working properly. All of a sudden, we heard a huge explosion—*Ker-whoom!* I thought the end of the world had occurred and immediately dived for cover. Steve never flinched. He was having more fun watching me run overtop the bark piles. He said later all he could see of me was elbows and a backside.

We found out that one of the airbags on the tractor had blown and we were out of service—just one of those days when I found myself in another conundrum. Oh, by the way, Steve and I talk often about conundrums and "comushions." You can buy them by the dozen at Krispy Kreme. Hmm.

There's never a time when Steve and I talk that we don't call each other names like Gooey Floodbottom, Pafoofnick, Stick in the Mud, Snicker Doodle, Goofball, Nut Ball or whatever other friendly names come to our minds. When he hangs up the phone with me, he always reminds me, "Don't forget to keep your powder dry and make sure you keep your flintlock out of your pocket when you're walking through water. And if you do get your powder wet, don't dry it out over a fire."

So it's no surprise that Steve played a role when in March of 2006 I felt like we needed to record a video project with our family. By this time, we had a dozen or so albums that we had released, and we were coming off two successful commercially produced albums—*Changed* and *I'll See You Home*. A couple of the songs were doing pretty well on the playlists of several Southern Gospel stations across the country, "Walkin' with the Lord" and "Old Fashioned."

It seemed like the timing was right to produce a concert DVD with our family, as an avenue to reach more people for Christ and get the story of restoration out to many more people.

Although there were considerable costs, we were meeting our financial needs. Still, I was talking about shooting a video. Trish said, "I don't know. That's pretty big. It's going to cost a lot of money."

I already knew that and had checked it out. It was going to cost $7,000 just for one night to have all the cameras and crew come in to do the video shoot, let alone the post production and duplication fees, which would total another $7,000.

Feeling very strongly that we should proceed with this, on faith I sent a $500 deposit and reserved a date in October 2006 for the shoot. We contracted with a production company based in Phoenix; the owner had produced many other video projects for groups such as Greater Vision, Signature Sound, The Cathedral Quartet, and The Talley Trio. Now all we needed was the money.

One afternoon in March of 2006, I received a phone call from Steve who asked, "What are you doing today?"

I said, "I'm sitting here in my office taking care of stuff I normally do."

He said, "If it's okay, I want to come out to your house. I want to help you open up an online savings account." I replied, "Steve, I can't keep any money in the savings account I already have. Why in the world would I want another one?"

He was insistent. He said, "Fran and I have been praying about this, and I want to help you open up an account. I'm going to contribute the first hundred dollars as seed money toward your new video project."

Well, we opened up the online savings account that afternoon, and on his own, Steve solicited sponsorships and donations from various people. By the time we shot the video, he had collected about $3,000. I was hoping for that amount, and we were real close.

The night of the video shoot was amazing. We were at the First Church of God in Meadville, and there were approximately 1,015 people in attendance. God's presence was there in a wonderful way.

I don't know where the money came from, but with the nearly $3,000 we had in the bank and $4,800 in the offering, plus video presales and hundreds of dollars in sponsorships from individuals who wanted to have a part in this project, we were able to generate the entire $14,200 needed to complete the project. One lady, who had already contributed $1,000, handed my wife a check that night for another $500. It was amazing!

When it was all said and done, our *Center Stage* DVD project from A to Z was one hundred percent paid for before it was ever released in April 2007.

The writer couldn't have gotten it any more right when he said it's not about I, me and mine or you, yours or you'uns, it's all about Him. None of these things has been about me. It's been a God thing from the beginning. And with help from the Lord, it will be about Him until the very end, whenever that time may come.

Now more than ever, I am convinced that what we do has been God ordained, and His hand of blessing is upon us. It is His will. It's a great feeling being in the place where you know you are meant to be. One night at a recent concert, I told one gentleman that when I am standing on the stage with my kids proclaiming Jesus Christ through my music, I feel fully alive.

CHAPTER 21

Songwriting

Questions I'm frequently asked are, "Where do the songs come from?" and "How do you write a song?" Well, for me, this is easy. It's just like breathing. It's a part of life. I have a creative mind, and I'm easily inspired by events, feelings, things I see, and places I go.

In the beginning years of our ministry, after becoming a Christian, I was filled with many new feelings. I was amazed at all God was doing in my life. I enjoy spending time just doodling on the keyboard. It is during these times that God will help me come up with new tunes. Most generally, when I hear a new tune, I hear the words at the same time—in four-part harmony. This is the way God gave me the words and music for songs like "Since Jesus Rescued Me," "In God's Time," "Old Fashioned," "U-Turn," and "Endless Praise," just to name a few.

My wife also has the ability to write poetically and has been a great help with adding a word or a second verse. Together, we have co-written many songs.

When I wrote "Old Fashioned," I was sitting in a camp meeting one afternoon while the evangelist preached on the topic of maintaining the old landmarks that our forefathers built and laid for us. One of her statements was, "I don't care what anybody else does or what other people do, I want to be an old-fashioned Christian!"

I about jumped off the seat. "Trish! I need pen and paper *now!*"

While I listened to the rest of the sermon, I was penning the words to "Old Fashioned." And about the time the sermon was over, I had the song pretty well written.

The chorus of the song is:

> *"I want to be an old-fashioned Christian and know I've been made whole*
> *I want to have the fire of God burning deep within my soul*
> *I don't care what people say or what the world may do*
> *I just want to be old fashioned and let the love of God shine through."*

Sometimes I will say, "I need to write a new song," but this is something you can't force. I've got to be inspired. One day a thought came to me, and I asked Trish if she'd ride along to Erie to Presque Isle. Sitting in the sand that night, watching the sun go down, I penned the words to "Endless Praise," which includes:

> *"I stand on the mountain and look to the sea*
> *My heart beats to the rhythm of endless praise*
> *Early in the morning and all through the day*
> *My heart beats to the rhythm of endless praise.*
>
> *(chorus)*
> *You are worthy, Lord, and greatly to be praised*
> *My heart sings a never-ending song of praise*
> *I will lift up my voice and proclaim your Holy Name*
> *As my heart beats to the rhythm of endless praise."*

A few years before my father passed away, near Christmastime we were visiting him and my mother in Worthington. Dad said, "Hey, I've got an idea about a song for you," and I was like, "Yeah, sure."

Next, my dad produced a paper with words scribbled only as Dad could write them—chicken scratch. When I read the words, amazingly, they all rhymed and were rhythmic. The words were,

> *"When I'm walkin'*
> *I get to talkin'*

Can't stop talkin'
When I'm walkin'
With the Lord

When I'm walkin'
I get to talkin'
Can't stop talkin'
When I'm walkin' with Lord

When I'm walkin'
I get to talkin'
Can't stop talkin'
When I'm walkin'
With the Lord

Walkin' and talkin'
And talkin' and walkin'
With the Lord.

Jeff was there with us that night, and we got around the piano in Mom and Dad's living room. Jeff said, "I think I hear a 12-bar blues rhythm with that song." And he started playing. Within seconds, we were singing what would become the chorus. It was awesome.

I said, "Dad, we've got a chorus for a new song. All we need is a verse."

A few weeks later, I was driving to Hermitage, and out of the blue, it hit me in the face:

"When I'm down in the valley
Or up high on the mountaintop
In the darkness of the midnight
Or when the sun is shining bright
I'm walkin' with my Jesus
I'm talkin' with my Lord
Well, I'm walkin' and talkin'
Talkin' and walkin' with the Lord."

From that, "Walkin' with the Lord" was born and became our second national radio release.

In the case of "Look What He's Done for Me," I was sitting in church listening to a sermon titled "Knots on the Family Tree of Christ." The message was about four women in the lineage of Christ whose pasts were questionable or had been tarnished in some way. The four the minister mentioned were Rahab, Tamar, Ruth and Bathsheba. And yet, God used these four women in the family lineage from which Christ would later come.

At the end of the message, the pastor said, "Why did God do this? God wanted to show us that He's a God of grace and mercy. He can use the worst of the worst to see His will accomplished."

Once again, it was, "Trish, I need pen and paper!" The entire song was built around the phrase, "He's a God of grace and mercy."

Sitting in my office and reflecting one day, I thought of the great transformation that had taken place in my life. And it hit me—I made a U-turn, from going as hard as I could in the wrong direction, to turning around and heading in the right one. With that thought in mind, the song "U-Turn" began to take shape.

The chorus says:

"I made a U-Turn on the highway of life
I changed my direction, now everything's all right
I turned around, and now I've got Heaven in my sight
Goin' to a city where there'll be no night
I'm not looking back, I will never turn around
I once was lost, but now I'm found
I was headed for destruction, but now my path is bright
Since I made a U-Turn on the highway of life."

Amazingly, when we released "U-Turn" to radio via the RadioActive Airplay/Caraway Media Group, it went to No. 1.

Our sound guy and I got the bright idea that we would film a video of "U-Turn" and put it on YouTube. So with camera and a script in hand, we embarked on this endeavor. One night, we decided we would go to Pittsburgh and shoot some video in the "not-so-good" section of the city. My friend Steve was also with us on this occasion.

So there we were, with Steve pulling Ray on a wooden cart so Ray could hold the camera steady. I acted out the song. They filmed me looking like I was coming out of a bar, and then walking down the street. At one point, I portrayed a man who was totally helpless, with no hope. I found myself between two large buildings, leaning against one and acting like I was crying while Ray shot the video. Please understand that it was nearly midnight as we were doing this. A man walked by and asked Steve what we were doing. Steve told him we were shooting a music video. The man replied, "That guy's really a good actor," which we all howled about later. It was nearly 3:00 a.m. when we left Pittsburgh.

These are just a few of the memories that I never would have had, had it not been for the fact that I made a U-turn.

The most recent song that the Lord gave me is entitled "Daddy's Pocket." You will be able to read about what inspired me to write the song and the story behind it in a later chapter. Out of all the songs I have written to date, "Daddy's Pocket" means more to me than all of them combined.

I've had people ask me, "Which is your best song?"

After thinking about it, my answer is, "The next one, the one that God hasn't inspired me to write yet."

I love people. I love visiting exciting places. I have asked God to allow me to be sensitive to the feelings of others in order to experience some of the emotions that they feel, and with each experience comes the possibility of a new song. But out of all of the songs I have written that have been successful, there are many starts that never made it onto paper.

I am confident that the best song I will ever write will be the praises that I sing when I'm finally kneeling in the presence of the King of Kings and Lord of Lords, the One who gave everything for me. I love Him with all of my heart, and the best is yet to come!

CHAPTER 22

Tales from the Road

Over the past two decades in our travels we often found ourselves in situations and out-of-the-way places wherein we stopped, scratched our heads, and wondered why we were really there. Sometimes, when we were invited into people's homes for meals, things went from strange to just plain weird. In a few of these situations, Trish told me if she thought about what she was eating, she'd get sick. I'd look at the people who were serving and say, "Well, if it ain't killed them yet, I guess we'll survive."

During the summers in the early years of our ministry, we sang at camp meetings. These meetings were usually ten days long, three services a day, in the mid- to late summer with mega humidity—uncomfortable, to say the least. To top it off, the singers generally ranked much lower in the pecking order than the other workers, and usually were put in a little cottage somewhere across the campground from wherever the restrooms were located. You could take a shower on one side of the campground, and by the time you walked back to your cottage on the other side, you needed another one. We had to be ready to lead the singing and sing specials three times a day, always looking our best. The camp evangelists split their time so each preached once one day and twice the next. Anyway, you get the picture.

At one particular camp meeting, we were called to fill in for a weekend when the regular song evangelists couldn't be there. We were already scheduled to be the regular song evangelists at the same camp for the full ten days the next year, so I'm glad we had the opportunity to go for that one weekend. Our eyes were opened, and we were able to prepare for what we would face the next summer.

The camp cook was from Jamaica. Talk about exotic food—I never knew you could come up with such concoctions. It was nothing like the good old country food that I was raised on. Where was Mom when we really needed her?

They showed us our cottage for the weekend. They'd told us earlier that it was cleaned and ready for us to move in. Well, when we walked in, it was one of the most bug-infested places I had ever seen. There were dead bugs on the floor, dead bugs on the bed, dead bugs on the windowsill—there were dead bugs every place you could see. Trish said, "How in the world are we going to manage this for the weekend?"

Somehow we did. God gave us grace. But before we moved in, we found brooms and dustpans and wiped things down. We tried to clean up as many of the dead bugs as we could and opened the windows to air the place out. Next year, on our list of supplies, we would be bringing a Shop-Vac, cleaning materials and our own sheets and towels.

We returned to the camp the following year for ten days. If you haven't figured out by now, I don't like bugs, especially spiders. In fact, I can have nightmares about spiders. Somehow, they grow bigger in my dreams. When I see a spider, its lifespan is cut short, as I refuse to be in the same locale.

One afternoon after service, we walked back to our cottage—oh, by the way, the cottage dimensions were approximately ten-by-twelve, and they expected five people to live in that space. Just outside the door, someone called, "Brother Keeling?" and I paused for a few minutes to talk to him. When we finished, I looked down at the cement blocks that were the cottage steps, and to my horror, I saw a huge brown spider, about as large a critter as you might expect to see in the movie *Arachnophobia*— not that I would ever watch that film anyway! I immediately began stomping my feet trying to kill the crazy thing and hoped that I had been successful.

After making my way into the cottage, I sat in the only chair in the cottage, an old armchair, to relax a little bit before next service. It was so dirty that Trish had to cover it with a sheet so we could sit on it. Bear in mind, this was the same day that the clothesline strung through the inside of the little cottage came down and all our dress clothes crashed to the floor.

So there I was, sitting and relaxing, contemplating in a meditative frame of mind about what songs I would lead and what we would sing for special music that evening, when suddenly I became aware that something was moving inside my pants in the area of my right knee. Something was crawling up my leg! The only picture that I could imagine in my mind was that huge, brown spider.

Let me tell you, it wouldn't have mattered to me if I'd been standing on the platform singing, or if the camp president or his wife, or even the President of the United States for that matter, were standing in front of me. Those pants were coming off! *And now.*

I jumped up, ripped off my suspenders, slapped my legs and those pants were a'comin' down! With a look of shock on her face, Trish yelled, "What! What! What's wrong?"

I don't like grasshoppers much either, but I sure was relieved to find it was only one of those that had crawled up my leg. *Phew!*

At another camp meeting, Jeffrey got sick while he was at the keyboard during an evening service. His face changed colors as he began to be nauseated. In spite of this, he was a real trooper. He knew I needed him to be at his post, and he hung right in there. When we were done singing the first special song, he walked off the platform, out of the tabernacle to a nearby ditch, and threw up. The poor guy. Then he returned through the side door, sat down and was ready to play the trumpet for the offertory. Over the years, our kids have sacrificed not only their time but much of themselves in order to be a part of our ministry.

Then there was the bat. During an afternoon service while singing at Pine Ridge Holiness Camp, it was almost offering time, and the Keeling boys, including myself, were scheduled to play for the offertory. One of the camp evangelists was a great man, Rev. Coy McGinnis. In addition to being an evangelist, he was a songwriter and wrote the song "He'll Furnish the Grace if You'll Furnish the Man." Brother Coy had a deep, manly voice.

Lynn, who was sitting on the platform beside me, nudged me and said, "Dad, there's a bat hanging in the rafters above us."

After I confirmed the bat was there, I nudged Brother Coy and said, "Brother McGinnis," and he said in that deep, manly voice, "Yes?" I said, "There's a bat hanging up in the rafters right above our heads. Do you see it?" As only as Brother McGinnis could say it, in a quiet rumble he said, "Sure enough." I always thought bats were nocturnal, but this bat must have been a different species.

The boys and I were playing "Keep on the Firing Line" as a piano trio, a song that has become a trademark of The Keelings. Everywhere we go, people want to hear The Keeling boys, along with Dad, play with five hands on the piano. It's silly the way we play it, but everybody seems to love it.

I don't know if it was the high frequency sounds we were playing on the upper end of the keyboard or what, But something woke that ol' bat up that afternoon, and he decided it was time for a solo flight.

It was hilarious! Heads ducked as the bat flew over. In fact, he flew down in front of the altar. As we were playing, Jeffrey said to me, "Was that the bat?" I said, "Yep. Just keep playing."

When we thought it couldn't get any funnier, a man came running down the center aisle, chasing the bat with a broom. We just kept on playing. About the time we were ready to finish the song, the other evangelist, who was sitting off to our left, got a songbook and whacked the bat, turned around, and gave the thumbs up sign. He was the hero.

During the years, Trish and the kids have had to put up with a lot. The worst thing we had to deal with was the heat. As long as I live, I'll never forget this one. It was a ten-day church camp near Kittanning, and during ninety percent of those ten days, the outside temperature simmered near ninety-five degrees with oppressive humidity. It was sweltering hot. Beads of sweat rolled off us all week long.

Normally, they would have put us in a workers' cottage that had air conditioning. However, due to health reasons, they had to give the workers' cottage to the camp president and his wife, which meant Trish, Lynn, and I were squeezed into a little cottage big enough for three, and the boys bunked across the path in another little cottage.

This camp started on a Thursday and went over two Sundays, ending on the second Sunday night. After the end of the first Sunday evening service, I came back to the cottage to find Trish lying on the bed wearing as little clothing as possible and sweating like crazy. With a groaning sigh, she said, "Randy, I can't take it anymore. I've *got* to have some relief."

As the old saying goes, "If Momma ain't happy, ain't nobody happy!"

Most people never realized all the work Trish handled behind the scenes. She may not have been up front singing, but she was running a hot iron in a closed-up space in all that heat making sure the kids and I looked our best as we sang for services three times a day. That's a lot to expect from any woman, let alone your wife.

I knew I had to do something, so I informed the camp president that I would be leaving in the morning and would not be back until I'd found a small air conditioner to put in the window. I finally located one in Butler, Pennsylvania. I missed the morning and afternoon services, but I was able to purchase a small air conditioning unit which I own to this day. It still works in my office. After installing it in the window of the cottage, momma was happy and we made it through the camp.

In addition to our other concerts, we did three church camps that summer that lasted ten days each with three services a day, for a total of ninety camp services, plus prayer meetings that you were expected to attend. And at one camp, we had the responsibility of leading the youth choir every morning at 9 a.m. and every evening at 6 p.m. And believe you me, our little friend who sat in the window keeping us cool was now a part of our family and traveled everywhere we went!

In the years to come, we ministered in just about every denomination that you can think of: Nazarene, Baptist, Church of Christ, Evangelical Congregational, United Methodist, Wesleyan Methodist, Friends, Pilgrim Holiness, Assemblies of God, Presbyterian, independent community churches, God's Missionary churches, Wesleyan Holiness, Seventh-day Adventist, Brethren in Christ, Bible Methodist, and Church of God—you name the flavor, we've been there.

The only time I've ever backed out of a concert was the time we were scheduled to sing in a church not far from Greenville. A women's group from the church had scheduled us, but two weeks before the concert, I received a call from the pastor. He wanted to inform us that we would not be able to sing any songs that made reference to the blood of Christ and/ or salvation and having a born-again experience. I politely listened, then told him that if we couldn't sing about any of those things, there would be nothing to sing about, and the concert was canceled.

Over the years, I can count on one hand the number of times we solicited a booking. We always felt it would be outside of the Lord's will to promote ourselves by calling and inviting ourselves. In our opinion, when the phone rang, regardless of the denomination, it was a sign from the Holy Spirit of where He wanted us to minister next, and that there was always a reason for our being called to a particular church.

In addition to counting on one hand the number of times we solicited a booking, the same is true for the number of times we have been canceled. If my memory serves me correctly, it's been just four times. Oddly, three of those were from the same pastor at the same church—and there never was going to be a fourth time. The beauty of this is that every time he canceled, we received a phone call from another church within hours wanting to book us on that very day. From that experience, I learned that God knew where He wanted us, and we were determined to follow His will.

A friend of mine begged us to go to New York City to do a concert at a small God's Missionary Church in Queens. The day we were there was miserably hot. In fact, with the humidity, the heat index was 105 degrees in the city.

We drove all night to get there, and my friend met us along Interstate 80, so he could ride with us. This was the first time that I'd been to New York City. I can't remember the year, but I do know the World Trade Center towers still stood in lower Manhattan, and we saw them as we crossed the George Washington Bridge. We traveled to NYC in the old Ford Aerostar—you know, the van that was possessed—pulling our ministry trailer through the city. After zigging and zagging our way through Manhattan, we made it to Queens.

The congregation of the church was made up of mostly Indians who immigrated to the United States by way of South America. Their customs were different than ours, and they didn't take too kindly to our early arrival. In fact, the pastor wouldn't let us in his house because we were a couple hours early. I guess in their culture, it's not polite to arrive early.

The kids were very young, very restless, and very thirsty. We ended up going to a nearby McDonald's to get drinks for them and wait until it was time to go back to the pastor's house. When we got back there again, it was the *right* time, and we were invited into his home. After introductions were made, we agreed to meet at the church at the prescribed time. We were not allowed to be early at the church either.

When we got to the church, we couldn't believe it. There were bars on the windows and one single aisle down the middle with old wooden benches on either side. Some of the women used handmade brooms to sweep the floor, as they were conducting vacation Bible school that evening. Talk about chaos! I never saw so many people packed into such small place. The size of the building was unbelievably small. We didn't think we needed all our sound equipment, but they insisted, and we obliged.

Finally, around 8:00 p.m., it was time for the service to start. We sang. And we sang. And we sang. In fact, we sang every song that we had in our repertoire and played every song that we knew on the trumpets. And when it was time, my friend who was preaching that evening got up to speak. After his message, the pastor of the church stood up and said, with a little bit of hesitation, "I theenk we wheel a'have thee Keelings to seng for us ageen." By now, it was after 10:00 p.m., and we didn't know what to sing other than some of the same songs over again, which is what we did.

Overall, it was a great night, and the people loved it. At about 11:00 p.m., the service was finally over, and we packed up our equipment. Then, they decided they wanted to give us a tour of New York City. We parked our van and trailer between two houses where they had a fence with a gate so it would be safe, and the plan was for all of us to get into one guy's fifteen-passenger van and tour the city.

While we stood on the street corner waiting to get in the van, I heard the popping sound of gunfire down the street. I hollered at Trish, "Hurry up and get the kids in the van! That's gunfire!"

Trish looked at me and said nonchalantly, "Oh Randy, that's somebody setting off fireworks."

I replied, "I know gunfire and that's gunfire."

As we were getting in the van and speeding away, the lower part of the street was beginning to swarm with police vehicles and flashing red lights. So much for the "fireworks."

So here we were on a midnight tour of Manhattan. Our driver took us through the Lincoln Tunnel and back and drove us down to Broadway and Times Square. I loved the city, and I was hooked.

We were packed in that van like sardines. There weren't enough seats for everyone, and the kids had to sit on the floor. I was sitting between the two front seats so I could see. We were speeding along, and this guy was driving like Mario Andretti. All of a sudden, everybody started screaming, "Tree! Tree! *Tree!*" We came to a screeching halt with just inches to spare from a huge oak tree that had fallen across on the road. Oh, by the way, I forgot to tell you, they'd had massive storms and wind damage in the area that day, and the downed tree was a result of the storms.

Somehow, we made it back to our van and trailer and began our journey back toward Hadley. Talk about a whirlwind trip—we'll never forget that one!

Since then, I have traveled back to New York City more times than I have fingers and toes. I have visited the Bowery Mission. I have been to the Brooklyn Tabernacle many times. If I could talk Trish into it, I would move to the city. New York City is like my second home.

Once, we got a call wanting us to sing in the state of Indiana. They said we wouldn't need to worry about lodging because they would put us up in a mission house. By this point in our ministry, we learned that when somebody says they're going to provide lodging for you, you hold your breath because you never know what conditions you're going to be in.

As for me, I can put up with most anything so long as it's clean. In fact, I can sleep on the floor, as long as it's clean and nothing will be crawling over me. And hopefully, when I take a shower, I find nothing growing in the tub.

When we arrived at our prearranged accommodations, it was one of *those* situations where you just tippy-toed everywhere and tried not to touch anything for fear of what would get on you. The place was a filthy, greasy mess.

The kitchen floor was greasy with grime ground into the linoleum. When you walked on it, you didn't dare take your shoes off because your socks would stick to the kitchen floor. We won't even discuss the bedrooms. The real kicker came when I looked in the bathroom. Let's not talk about that either.

As CEO of the family, I declared that it was time for a family meeting.

We searched the house for a local phone book. We started looking for numbers for hotels in the area, only to find out that the only phone book in the house was from Florida, and we were in the state of Indiana. Thank God for cell phones. I called information and asked if there were any hotels in our area, and to my relief, Comfort Inn came to the rescue. We didn't want to offend the people who were next door, but we knew we couldn't stay there. I don't know if they heard our van leaving but I know that we sneaked out of the house a whole lot more quietly than we arrived! Just another one of *those situations.*

There have been times when I have been speechless, but nothing made me more so than the night during a concert when a woman hollered out and said, "Will you sing "The Lighthouse" for $100?" I didn't know what to say. I'd never been asked that question before. And she hollered it out right toward the end of one of our concerts.

I told her, well, we'll sing another song that another lady requested prior to yours. I told the crowd that it could be a very interesting night if we started singing all of our request songs for $100. We could be here for a long time!

Minutes later, we sang her song and true to her word, when the concert was over, she came up and handed me five twenty-dollar bills. A few weeks later at another concert, the same lady did it again. Only this time, it was a $100 bill. I could really get used to this. The third time it happened, I guess we didn't sing it quite as well because she only gave us $50.

Not long ago, while singing a concert with Jeff and Sherri Easter and The Stevens Family at Packard Music Hall in Warren, Ohio, that same "crazy" lady asked us again to sing "The Lighthouse," and this time, we got nothing.

Then, there is Ray, our soundman. Ray Young has been our sound technician for more years than I can remember. He's one of the best in the business with an associate's degree from Penn Technical Institute in Pittsburgh. He's worked in the field of bioelectronics and in hospital maintenance for years. Put it this way: Ray is kind of a cross between a computer geek, techie nerd, and MacGyver. I've told Ray many times that if we were in a survival situation, I'd definitely want him on my side.

When Ray was younger, he worked a short stint after college for the National Security Agency as a computer technician. You name it, Ray can figure it out. I have seen him fix things on the fly, make things work, and make something out of nothing with only a couple of tools in his hand.

Ray is the only man in Greenville who would be brave enough to don a set of tree climbers and a harness so he could climb the tallest tree in his backyard to hang a string of green LED lights—just to mark his property. Ray also is always working on projects that will take him off the electricity grid. He has solar panels on the outside of his garage, an inverter and batteries in his basement, and anything he can make something useful out of. One of Ray's finer moments was when he built a paraplane from scratch using parts he had found while "Dumpster-diving," a piece of titanium, and other components he purchased.

When it came time for the maiden voyage of his paraplane, it was a crash-and-burn situation. Ray did make it several feet into the air, and thankfully, when he crash-landed, other than his wounded pride and a busted propeller, he survived. If you go to Ray's basement, the broken propeller still hangs on the wall as a symbol of his heroic efforts.

In the old days, we recorded music in Ray's basement, and he was always in the process of building a new gizmo or gadget. At one time, he was collecting motherboards and circuit boards from computers. To this day, one of the walls in his basement is decorated with his collection.

Ray is just like family. Even though he's nearly sixty, he's like one of the kids, and we love having him around.

One Sunday morning in Robertsville, Ohio, Ray was not able to be with us. As we were setting up our equipment preparing for sound checks, I realized that the position of the knobs on the soundboard had been changed. Ray had been running sound for us the previous week and had forgot to put all the knobs back where they belonged. I was in a pickle. What in the world were we going to do? Jeffrey reminded me recently of the way that I reacted as I was frantically trying to figure out how to make the soundboard work, and the only words that were coming out of my mouth were a very lengthy, extensive, *"Raaaaaaaaaaaaaaay! Oh, dear Jesus, please help us. Ray, what did you do?"*

Ray has since taught Trish how to run sound, so that in his absence, I can restrain my emotions.

Our greatest reward from the ministry is hearing from the people whose lives have been touched. I think of the woman from Norfolk, Virginia who wrote me a letter after hearing the song "I Won't Have to Cross Jordan Alone" on the Bible Broadcasting Network and how it ministered to her as she was suffering from loneliness.

One night a woman said, "I have been listening to you guys for a long time. Randy, I have heard your testimony, and I want you to know that because of your testimony and the testimony of your family, I have quit drinking, I have accepted Christ, and now am attending AA." She said, "If you can do it, so can I."

Just a couple of days ago, I received the sad news that this woman, our friend Debbie Wells, passed away. We will miss seeing you at our concerts, but we will see you again in heaven. So glad you made a U-Turn.

This reminds me of a phrase from a song we used to sing that says if just one more soul came forward and accepted Christ, it would be worth every struggle and every mile if it rescued just one more soul.

At a concert in Grove City, Pennsylvania, a man who had been backslidden for years came forward and rededicated his life to Christ. We recently saw that man, and he's still doing well. That was the same night that my then-future son-in-law came to the altar as well. Praise God from whom all blessings flow!

Every day, we receive cards, letters, and notes of encouragement from people all across the country whose lives have been touched by the music and by the spirit in which it was presented. Just the other day, one man said to me, "Randy, other groups entertained me, but The Keelings ministered to me." That is the greatest compliment we could ever receive.

The long road we have traveled has taken us from the Queens in New York City to Maryland, Virginia, West Virginia, North Carolina, Tennessee, Indiana, Ohio, Kentucky, and our home state of Pennsylvania. We have sung to groups of as few as 25 people to 1,500 to thousands. And in all of the comments that people make to us, the common theme is that The Keelings are real, and they live what they believe and what they sing about.

Where this long road will take us, only God knows, but the best is yet to come.

The Keelings, 2013, standing from Left to Right, Pat Willaman,
Lynn Willaman, Randy Keeling & Doug Keeling
Seated, Jeff Keeling

The Keeling Family, 2011, standing from Left to Right, Jeff Keeling,
Pat Willaman, Randy Keeling, Trish Keeling & Doug Keeling
Seated from Left to Right: Hannah Keeling, Lynn Willaman & Nancy Keeling

The Keelings music group in 2011
From Left to Right, Jeff Keeling, Doug Keeling, Randy
Keeling, Lynn Willaman & Pat Willaman

This is our first Grandson, Jacob Ross Willaman
whose birth was written about in the book,

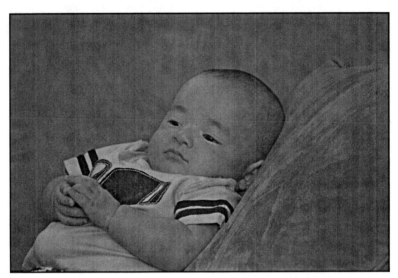

This is a photo of my second grandson, whose coming was mentioned, his arrival was after the book was completed.

This is Aaron Josiah Willaman, born in November 2013, after the book was completed. The family keeps growing.

The Keelings in action along with Jeff & Sheri Easter and
Stevens Family at Packard Music Hall in Warren, OH

CHAPTER 23

The Kids

Of all the treasures I possess in this world, the greatest is that of being a father. The greatest gift that God has given Trish and me is our three children, Jeffrey, Doug, and Lynn. I cannot help being a little prejudiced, nor do I want you to think me braggadocious, but in my opinion, God couldn't make kids any better.

As you have already read in previous chapters, I have not been, nor will I ever be the picture of perfection when it comes to fathering. But I have tried to be an old dog that can learn new tricks. I guess that's just another way of saying I've tried to learn from my many mistakes.

But enough about me—let's talk about the kids.

Jeff

In my opinion, Jeff is a bright star. At four and a half years old, he could play the piano by ear and already was putting songs together. He started his piano studies at age seven. I remember telling him, "One of these days, you're going to be a phenomenal player."

If you think I'm prejudiced toward my son, you're right. If you listen to any of his recordings and watch him take command of the keyboard as he performs, you will know that this kid has a true gift from God. Many nights after our concerts, people come to me and say, "I can't believe it. Anthony Burger lives on through your son's hands." I can't take any credit for this, but the facts are the facts. When it comes to Southern Gospel pianists, this kid is at the top.

Jeffrey, now twenty-nine years old, graduated from Commodore Perry High School and Thiel College with honors. Now, in addition to playing piano for The Keelings, he's employed at his old high school as the principal.

For Jeff, life has been an educational journey. After receiving his bachelor's degree from Thiel College, he went on to receive his master's degree from Youngstown State University. Realizing that he wanted to have a greater impact on his students, he then got his principal's certificate from Gannon University in Erie, Pennsylvania. Currently, he is working online toward his Ed.D. in education leadership from Liberty University in Lynchburg, Virginia.

Jeff takes his work in the field of public education very seriously. Even though God has regretfully been removed from the classrooms of our public schools, Jeff feels that he can make a difference and does his best to be a living Christian example to his students and to the rest of the faculty.

When it comes to music, Jeff is a natural. When he was in the fifth grade, he took up the trumpet, which he continued to play throughout high school. He was first chair trumpet in the concert band and was a major force in the jazz band. At the senior band concert, he won the prestigious Louis Armstrong Jazz Award, a national award for jazz musicianship.

One thing that used to annoy me was when I heard him referring to his mother as "Pat." I would observe him picking his mother up off her feet while she was standing in the kitchen and he would say, "And how's Pat doing today?" I thought he was being disrespectful but soon found out it was just his little pet name, showing his affection for his mother. I remember all the little pecks he would give her on the cheek, his way of showing his love for his mother. Every now and again, he still says, "And how's Pat doing?" and Mom just blushes.

In music, the kid is just awesome. He understands music better than people who have studied professionally all their lives. When he sits down to play the piano, there's something special about the way he puts things together. His chord structuring and the things he hears are outstanding.

Not only does he play the piano, but he will usually make music with whatever instrument he picks up. He has become accomplished on the electric guitar, acoustic guitar, bass, brass and percussion.

Jeff's duties for The Keelings include being the keyboardist, trumpeter, arranger and singing the bass part. In the recording studio, he also uses his talents on the guitar and drums, which have become a couple of his favorite instruments.

Jeff was originally certified to teach English, but one day I told him he should challenge the PRAXIS exam for music. If he passed, it would certify him to teach that as well. I told him if he took the test, I would pay for it. He said, "Are you sure you want to do this? What if I fail?" My reply was, "Well, I guess I could waste my money on a lot worse things." Needless to say, he did not let me down. He passed, and is now certified to teach music.

Jeff is respected most everywhere he goes. His students speak highly of him. Although he is tough on them, they respect him because he's a man who sticks to his convictions and does extra things to try to help them.

When he graduated from high school, Jeff ran a write-in campaign and got elected at age eighteen to the Board of Education for the Commodore Perry School District. He served until he later applied for and accepted the position of English teacher. When Jeff resigned from the board, younger brother Doug was appointed to fill his seat.

While Jeff was at Thiel College, he met a young woman named Hannah Smith. She was from Elderton, Pennsylvania, a town not too far from my hometown of Worthington. During their college years, their relationship continued to develop, and today they have been married for four years. Hannah has proved herself to be a great daughter-in-law. She's a great cook, a wonderful artist, and she teaches eighth-grade English in Saegertown, Pennsylvania.

In my heart, I know that it has been Jeffrey's desire to make a difference in the world, and that he is doing. One of the things I'm most proud of is the fact that he accepted the Lord as his Savior at an early age and has endeavored to serve Him throughout his life. I probably don't tell him enough how much I love him, but he has been a rock and a source of stability for his dad. He is the kind of son that every dad would desire to have.

Doug

Ol' Doug, what a talented son. He's just like a cuddly teddy bear. We recognized early that he had a real gift for creativity and art. When it comes to graphic design, he is one of the best of the best. We are absolutely proud of him.

Not only is he gifted with art, but he's got a great ear for music. He also studied piano in his early years and then in the fifth grade, he took up the trumpet and continued playing throughout high school. During his junior year, he actually outdid his brother, as he received the national Louis Armstrong Jazz Award, which typically goes to a senior. But that year, there was no senior who could match him. Then, in his senior year, Doug won the coveted John Phillip Sousa Award for musicianship. As far as we know, Doug is the only one in the history of Commodore Perry High School Band to have received both national awards.

When Doug was in the first or second grade, we were called in for a parent-teacher conference. It was discovered that Doug was not being challenged enough, and it was recommended that he be tested for the gifted program. As a result of this, we discovered that Doug was in the top two percent of all the kids in the United States, and he was placed in the gifted and accelerated learning program at school. All through elementary and high school, he maintained a straight 4.0 GPA.

Talk about a proud moment! I could hardly contain myself when he got up to make the salutatorian speech. Doug referred to his old dad in his speech, and that was a touching moment. He talked about doing your best in life and what he saw me do when the kids brought report cards home.

If there was a grade that maybe wasn't as good as it should have been, I'd say, "Listen, can you look me in the eye and tell me that you did your best? Is this the best you can do?" And if they could tell me that was the best they could do, then I'd say, "Get your chin up because all I ever expect from you is your best. Whatever it is that you do, just do the best you can. I don't expect you to walk on water. If you can do it better, then do better. But if this is your best, then I'm OK with that."

Doug referred to this in his speech when he said, "I remember my dad saying many, many times, 'At the end of the day, if you did your best, then you can be proud.'" I'll never forget that moment as long as I live.

Unfortunately, today there are so many moms and dads who push their kids to the limit. This often results in frustrated and bitter kids.

During his junior year of high school, Doug got hired on as an intern in graphic design at Bucks Fabricating, just down the road from our home. They saw an ad he did for the high school yearbook, and they hired him on the spot. Doug worked at Bucks during his junior and senior year and through his first year of college.

Speaking of college, Doug also attended Thiel College in Greenville where he graduated as valedictorian with a double major in Web Development and E-Commerce.

Today, Doug is married to the former Nancy Lengauer who is an elementary teacher at Oakview Elementary School in Sandy Lake, Pennsylvania. Nancy has proven herself to be a great daughter-in-law as well, and she's a good cook.

While they were dating, I would often tease her, "Nancy, don't bother coming to visit unless you bring some of that buffalo chicken dip and Tostitos Scoops." She would laugh and although she didn't bring it every time, she made sure that I had a readily available supply. They always say that the way to a man's heart is through his stomach. This also works in the case of winning over a future father-in-law.

Soon to be twenty-seven, Doug is an entrepreneur as the owner of Keeling Design & Media at www.DougKeeling.com, where he has built up a sizable clientele, developing websites and creating graphic images for clients across the country. Recently, one of his designs appeared on the television stations in the Youngstown, Ohio, area on an advertisement for auto sales. He said it was pretty cool to see his work on the screen.

When it comes to a work ethic, Doug's self-discipline and dedication are incomparable. He's the kind of guy who does his best to fit it in no matter what he's asked to do. Sometimes, I must admit he can get a little disgusted and sigh when I ask him for the next favor.

Doug accepted the Lord as his Savior at a young age and continues to serve Him to this day. A touching moment happened one night before he was married. I was standing back in my bedroom and Doug came to the door, and he said, "Dad, I was acting like a jerk last week."

And I said, "Well, you definitely seemed a little stressed out."

He said, "I just want you to know I'm sorry."

I hugged him and said, "You're forgiven," and we moved on. I'm sure glad we have been able to keep an open line of communication between us.

With The Keelings, Doug sings baritone and plays the bass and trumpet. In our recording studio, he is our engineer and does all the brass orchestrations which has taken our music to its highest level of professionalism yet. This has gotten the attention of some of the best engineers in the business, who noted that our music sounds live, as he will often put eight or nine trumpets, a complete brass ensemble, behind us. With his unique ability to hear parts, Doug uses this gift to break down all the harmony parts, making songs easier for us to learn. And, of course, he designs the album covers, the press posters, the advertisements, the tickets, and serves as webmaster for www.thekeelings.org.

Lynn

Lynn is a special gift. I realized when I was teaching her how to drive just how old I was getting. The reality hit me that this was my little girl.

All through Lynn's childhood, there were those moments where I really wasn't sure if I was that important in her life. You know how it is with girls—they're different than boys. Some days they think you're great, and other days, you're not so hot. During her formative years, Lynn's mother was very important in her life and still is to this day. But I did my best to be a part of her life and show her that I loved her. Today, Lynn and I have a special relationship. I have found out that of all of my kids, she's the one who is most like me, which is probably why we had a few of *those* moments.

One evening while at McDonald's, I had done something to offend Lynn, who was only about age three. She was not happy with her father. As we were getting ready to walk out the door, I asked her, "Lynn, do you love your daddy?" and as serious as she could be, with tears in her eyes, she said, "I don't know. I'm just not sure." I told her that we wouldn't be able to leave until she told me she loved me. She was stubborn and we stood there for a while. Then finally, whether by force or out of the goodness of her little heart, she told me that she did.

One day, when Lynn was around four years old, I received a frantic call on my cell phone from my wife, telling me that Lynn had just been in a bicycle accident. At that moment, I was in Boardman, OH attending a company meeting and was not immeadiately able to come home. The boys had been riding their bikes up and down the hill that went through the trailer park where we lived. They would pedal to the top and then, you guessed it, fly back down the hill. Monkey see, monkey do, and Lynn had to do it too.

She followed the example of her big brothers, only Lynn, just a few feet from our driveway, flew over the handlebars of her bike. This resulted in a severe case of road rash to her legs, hands and especially to her face. Trish kept telling me on the phone, "Honey, she might not ever look the same again." Even her lip had skidded onto the road, and there was dirt ground in between her teeth and under her lower lip.

Believe you me, Lynn got a lot of attention during that time. Everybody was babying her. Jeffrey would go up and say, "Aw, how you doing?" trying to be the big brother comforting his little sister. The wounds healed and she's a beautiful young lady today. She's a special daughter with a heart of gold and would do anything to help others.

I found out recently that while she was in high school, a young man touched her in an inappropriate way. Had I known about this, I would have knocked his head off. However, Lynn handled it like a champ. She got his attention. She grabbed his wrists, looked him in the eye and said, "If you ever touch me like this again, I will report it to the principal. I would not allow my boyfriend to touch me in this way, and you keep your hands off of me, period." All through her life, she proved to be a respectable young lady. I've been real proud of her.

Throughout high school, Pat Willaman had been Doug's best friend, and he had visited our home several times as he and Doug would get together and do what kids do. At that time, I thought he was okay, and he seemed like a normal young man. However, when I found out that he had asked Doug how I would feel if he asked my daughter out on a date, my opinion of him immediately changed. No one would be good enough for my daughter! The rules of engagement just changed—not to mention that Lynn was only seventeen at the time and Pat was a few years older.

After much pleading and attempts to convince me otherwise by Lynn, I finally consented that Pat could come over to the house. However, I was going to lay down the law, and it would be my way or the highway. When

Pat came to the house for the first time under *new* circumstances, I closed the door from my office to the living room and set it up so Pat would have to come through the office to get into the house. When he came in, I shook his hand very businesslike and offered him a chair in my office.

I proceeded to lecture him on the fact that out of all the gifts God had given me, my kids were the greatest gift. He should know I would be willing to die in a heartbeat to save or protect one of my kids. I wanted him to know that if he was with my daughter, it would be a hands-off-the-merchandise situation only. No touch! And if he was going to take my daughter out, Doug had to go along!

I did my best to see if I could make him cower. However, his desire to be with my daughter was greater than his fear of me. We agreed, shook hands, and then I invited him to go into the living room to see Lynn.

Shortly after, in my haste to leave for another engagement, I hurriedly made my way outside to my Jeep, not realizing that Pat had parked really close behind me with his Ford Explorer—and it was very dark outside. About right now, you can imagine what happened. I put the old Jeep in reverse, hit the accelerator, and *wham!* I smashed into his front bumper with my rear one.

So there I was, this big tough guy breathing out threats to this guy who's wanting to see my daughter, now walking with my tail between my legs and knowing that I'm going to be eating a very huge portion of humble pie. We have laughed about this on many occasions since then, and Pat has proven to be a trustworthy son-in-law. In many ways, he is just like a third son.

Today, Pat is employed as a design engineer with Joy Mining and Machining in Franklin, Pennsylvania. It's such a blessing having a son-in-law who is an engineer. I have found him to be quite useful in reading manuals, as engineers read all the details, which I hate to do. When he was helping me install a backhoe on my tractor, it was really cool: He read the manual; I turned the wrenches.

As I mentioned in a previous chapter, Lynn was instrumental in bringing healing to the family, coming after the loss of Darren, Doug's twin brother, and the fact that she was born on my sister Connie's birthday. But beside that, she's just a ray of sunshine.

Lynn is also talented in music. By age three, she was singing solos at many of the Keeling concerts, and at age ten, she joined the elementary band as a flute player. She continued playing it through high school in the symphonic band, and then she played the tenor sax in the jazz band.

For four years in a row she won outstanding alto in the middle school and high school choir. Then, like her brothers, she was listed in "Who's Who Among American High School Students." All three kids were members of the National Honor Society. And to boot, she also won the John Phillip Sousa band award during her senior year.

Lynn also accepted the Lord as her Savior at a young age and has continued to serve Him to this day. After graduating from Penn State University as a physical therapist assistant, she married her best friend and my son-in-law, Mr. Pat Willaman, you know, the one whose bumper I backed into.

A touching moment for Lynn and me came about three weeks before her engagement. Our relationship had been somewhat strained, as I was having a very difficult time accepting the fact that my baby would be leaving home, and I was only forty-four years old. I was too young to have all of my kids out of the house, especially my baby girl.

One night in my office, I made one last attempt to see if I could talk her out of getting married, and I will never forget the look in her eye or the words that she said. With tears streaming down her cheeks, she said, "Dad, I love him." But it was the look in her eye that made me change. I could see that she was madly in love, and I would never be able to stop the inevitable. They were meant for each other. God was in it. It was His will.

When Pat asked me for my daughter's hand, I said, "Pat, I'm not going to fight this. I can see that this was meant to be. My daughter loves you. And it would appear that you love her. But you need to remember, where I come from, this is a lifelong commitment. Pat, this is my daughter, and I will remind you again that I would die tomorrow to protect her. So I want your word that you're going to take care of her, protect her, love her and, second to God, keep her first in your life."

A few weeks later, she came home with a piece of the rock, and the rest is history. For The Keelings, Lynn sings tenor and helps in various ways after each concert. One year as we were practicing for our Christmas concert, Pat stood in the living room singing along. I never knew he could sing. After moving a little closer to him, I realized he could do more than just carry a tune in a bucket. He was quite good, and I said, "Where have you been all my life?" Thus, before they were married, Pat became a very important part of the group and from then until now, he has been a great help and continues to sing with the family at each concert.

On July 30, 2012, at 3:42 in the afternoon, our first grandchild, Jacob Ross Willaman, was born after thirty-six hours and twelve minutes of labor. The most beautiful sound that I've ever heard, better than all the songs or melodies I've heard, was the sound of my grandson crying for the first time. I am truly a blessed man.

Let me take you to 3:30 p.m. on the day Jacob was born, just twelve minutes prior to his birth. I had planted myself outside the door of the delivery room. Trish and Pat were in the room with Lynn and the medical staff. I could hear Lynn groaning with every labor pain. She kept saying, "Pat, I can't do any more." And he calmly assured her, "Yes, you can. We'll do it together."

As the drama was unfolding, one of the nurses ran out of the room to the nurse's station just down the hall from where I was standing. I heard her page for two other doctors to get to the delivery room where my daughter was, *now*. At that moment, I knew all was not well. One of the other nurses told me that as the baby was coming through the birth canal, his heart rate was rapidly dropping, and they were afraid they would have to perform resuscitative measures.

The next eighteen minutes seemed like a lifetime. All I could do was pray. I told God, "I don't want to lose my daughter, and I don't want to lose my grandson. I've never asked You for much, but I sure would appreciate if You would grant this request."

As I stood on the other side of the door, Trish and I exchanged a series of texts:

3:27 p.m.—From Trish: "He's almost here."

Randy: "Yep, I'm right outside the door, praying."

Trish: "Can't come in for quite a while."

Randy: "I understand. Just worried."

3:42 p.m.—I heard the baby cry.

3:45 p.m.—(After waiting way too long for word) Randy: "He's here and ok?"

Trish: "Perfect!!"

Randy: "Praise the Lord"

About thirty minutes later, when I finally got to lay eyes on him for the first time and to hold him, I was overcome with emotion. Truly, one of the greatest blessings God has given me. I have been teasing Lynn since, "Lynn, hurry up and get him house-broken so I can take him and teach him all the manly things."

All the kids are unique. They all get along. The two boys are like best friends, and the daughters-in-law get along and somehow manage to put up with my quirkiness. When the boys were younger, they would put on a tape or DVD to watch together before bedtime. Today, they have Ford Mustangs that are identical, other than the color. One is gold and one is silver. Both are detailed identically with a design that Doug created.

I remember telling them around the dinner table, "Kids, our family is all we have in life. All the material things we have matter nothing. The only thing we can take with us when we leave this world is our family. You've got your brother. You've got your sister. You've got your mom and your dad. This is it. This is us. This is The Keelings. We've got to stick together, stick up for each other, love each other and help each other. When the world around us is falling apart, never forget that we're a family. We stick together."

Many times I have told the kids, "Remember, if one of you is in need and you have the means to help the other out, do it, and do it willingly and unselfishly. If you see your sister in need, or vice versa, don't be bitter over who may have more, because that won't matter in the end. It's about family. Never allow jealousy or bitterness to destroy your relationship with each other."

As you know, my dad was adopted, and our last name should have been Tarr. So we're starting off a new family tree. Basically, it's a whole new group, a whole new family. We fight for each other. We stand up for each other. We'll defend each other. We'll fight to the death for each other if we have to.

We've had our share of bad times, disagreements, and pain. But there is an unbreakable bond of love between us, and I pray to God that it will never change.

These are my kids, my greatest gift from God.

CHAPTER 24

Family Values

By now, you know that I am a very unworthy man. But I am thankful that God could take a mess like mine and somehow make something good of it.

The older I become, the more I understand that last night's concert or Sunday morning's message could be my last. I also understand that every time I see my kids could be the last. I am not naïve about the fact that every day is a precious gift from God. Just as God gave Trish and the kids to me, He can take them all away. Every day we have together and every concert we sing together is a gift from God. It's a dream come true.

The title of a recent message said, "Live Today Like There's No Tomorrow." I tell the kids all the time, "Be careful. Always be watching." And most importantly, "Be ready." I have done my best to impart to them the wisdom from the tough lessons that I've learned. When they ask me for advice, I encourage them to pray about it, to read their Bibles, and to ask God what He thinks about it. The world says trust your heart, trust your instincts, trust your gut. But I say they're wrong. We must put our faith and trust in God. What does He say? What does He think? And then be obedient. See Proverbs 3:5-6.

When Jeff talked to me before he got engaged, I used this analogy: "When you were little, we never let you cross the road without holding your hand. We were always there to make sure you were okay. Then, when you got a little older, we would let your cross the road, but you always crossed the road with Mom or Dad by your side without holding your hand. We were there just to keep our eyes on you.

"But now as an adult, you will have to cross this road by yourself. We've done our best to teach you to look both ways before crossing. I've tried to teach you the ways of God and to be smart about life and to make good decisions. So son, you're going to have to cross this road on your own."

"However, if you get hit, if you get knocked down, Dad and Mom are going to be there to help pick you up. I'm going to try to do my best until I'm out of this world to be there for you. I don't have much materially, but I've tried to instill in you the abilities to think smart, be sharp, make the best of everything, look for opportunities, be loyal, and build relationships that are lasting."

Both Trish and I did our best to help the kids understand that in God's eyes, they are special, and the most important thing they can do is to give their lives wholly to Him. We taught them the value of going to church every Sunday and making God number one in their lives.

During all the years in our travels, we attempted to set an example and raise the standard high on remembering and keeping the Sabbath day. Of all the commandments that are listed in the Bible, this one commandment—"Remember the Sabbath day, to keep it holy" (Exodus 20:8-11)—is mentioned more times than any other.

Nothing grieves me more than to see people desecrate the Lord's Day with every other activity than worship—sports, hobbies, unnecessary work, family get-togethers, shopping excursions. It's as if Sunday is just another day. But God is still the same. He hasn't changed. Don't get me wrong. I understand making exceptions if the "ox is in the ditch." We have to be reasonable. But my problem is when we fill up our Sundays with unnecessary things and put Jesus on the shelf.

Right about now, some of my contemporaries who may be reading this book are thinking, "Randy, that was just for the people of the Old Testament age. And besides that, the Jewish Sabbath was Saturday."

I would like to remind you that God rested on the seventh day of creation, setting the example, knowing full well that His creation, man and woman, would need one day a week to rest and worship Him. Now, I know today we worship on the first day of the week, Sunday, because the Christian Sabbath is on the first day of the week as we celebrate the Resurrection at each Sunday worship service. And because He lives, we can face tomorrow.

Even to this day, at our concerts on Sundays, we use the honor system. People can take home whatever number of CDs they wish, with the understanding that they will send us a check or money order for the amount owed within the next couple days. We choose to honor God on Sunday, the Christian Sabbath, and will not accept payment for any CDs taken on that day. We may have lost a few sales, but God has made up the difference, and we have honored Him in the process.

One night at a high school band concert, the director complained to me that our kids were not allowed to go on the school band trips. He said, "Randy, I really need your boys." And I said, "Sir, the reason my boys don't go is because you always travel over a Sunday and we choose to honor God in our home on Sundays. So if you want my boys and my daughter to go, you need to arrange the band trip so it doesn't interfere with Sunday worship. Don't tell me that you can't change the minds of school administration." While the boys were in high school, the band trips were rescheduled and arranged for a Thursday, Friday, and Saturday. The kids were allowed to go and God was honored.

A well-known television evangelist wrote in an article that he was at a restaurant on Sunday and asked the young man who was his waiter, "Son, do you ever go to church?" And the young man replied, "No sir, I can't go to church because I'm always here waiting on the people who are coming home from church."

The evangelist was convicted in his heart and said, "The Bible says we are not supposed to be a stumbling block to our brothers and our sisters. By the grace of God, I will not be a hindrance ever again to your being able to attend Sunday worship."

That was the last time he ever ate out in a restaurant on a Sunday. Our actions affect others just as our inactions affect others.

What has been amazing to me is that there are Ten Commandments, but this is the one that we like to say no longer matters. Oh yes, we keep the other nine, but Jesus said, "If you love me, you keep my commandments." I wonder what the response of many people will be on judgment day when they stand before God. What excuse will they give? What answer will they give concerning placing the things of this world above God? Jesus gave everything on the cross for us, so why is it so difficult to honor Him *one* day a week?

In light of this, in all the years of our travel, never once did we eat at a restaurant on Sunday. Rather, we chose to honor God and took our meals with us. Trish always made sure that we had a well-stocked ice chest with plenty to eat while traveling.

Additionally, we always did our best to pre-plan our ministry travels to avoid having to purchase gasoline on Sunday. You say, "How did you do this when you were traveling so many hundreds of miles?" It's called pre-planning. We always filled up the tank the night before, and we carried gasoline with us. Or we would ask the church where we were singing if they could have a can of gas waiting for us, so we could put it in the van before we started home. On a few very long trips, we purchased prepaid gas cards to use, so we would not have to make any transaction inside the station and could handle everything at the pump without having to make anyone serve us. While traveling home on Sunday nights, if we knew we were getting low on gas, we would find a place to pull over, take a nap, and wait until after midnight.

One night while traveling home from Binghamton, N.Y., we were running on fumes. I had already put in the extra ten gallons I had taken along, and we made it back as far as Erie, Pennsylvania, with the gas gauge sitting on empty. I made a phone call to a friend of mine in Meadville and asked if he had any gas. All he had was about two gallons, and we were still in Erie, about 40 miles away. Call it crazy, call it what you want, we honored God. When we pulled into his driveway in Meadville, the van was still running, and the two gallons got us home. Our kids saw this. They were learning by our example.

While I'm on the subject of honoring God, I guess this would be a great opportunity to mention tithing. Even though my home life as a child may have been dysfunctional, my mother always said, "If you pay your tithe, you'll never go hungry." In effect, she was saying, "If you honor God, He will honor you."

Through the years, we made it a habit to tithe a minimum of ten percent of our gross income to the Lord, and in many cases went well beyond that, for the Lord loves a cheerful giver. Doug argued the value of tithing in a public school debate and won the top prize in the competition.

Malachi 3:8-10 says, "Will a man rob God? Yet ye have robbed me. But ye say wherein have we robbed thee? In tithes and in offerings. You are cursed with a curse for ye have robbed me, even this whole nation. Bring ye all the tithes into the storehouse that there may be meat in my house and prove me now herewith, saith the Lord of hosts, if I will not open you the windows of Heaven and pour you out a blessing that there shall not be room enough to receive it."

Even at our lowest points financially, our tithe was paid first before anything else. Our kids saw this, and they learned by our example. From the time I was converted, we did everything we could to instill in our children these two values of honoring God by keeping the Sabbath day holy and willingly paying our tithe.

While attending junior high school, my daughter needed a new flute. We did not have the money to purchase an expensive one for her, so my advice was, "Save all of the money you make on the weekends singing, and you will be able to buy a new flute."

Lynn was so proud when we traveled to World of Music in Erie and purchased a brand new Yamaha professional model flute. Complete with a gold mouthpiece, it was a beautiful instrument.

During our ten-year anniversary concert, Lynn was featured in a flute solo. Before she played, I mentioned that she had purchased the flute with money she had saved. After the concert, a man came and asked me how much the new flute cost. After being pressed, I reluctantly told him, and he told me that he would be sending a check in the mail to Lynn to reimburse her savings account for the amount she had spent on the flute. A week later, that check arrived—for $1,000, and Lynn had learned a lesson that you can't out-give God.

One day the phone rang, and the gentleman on the phone told me of a man who had a car that he wanted to give away to a young man who was a Christian. In my mind I was thinking, "Yeah, right. No one gives away a car. What's the catch?" So I took the information, and for a week, I did nothing with it, thinking it was too good to be true.

A week later, the same man called back and told me the same story. He said that he had Doug in mind, and that I should call the man with the car. Doug was only fifteen. We had already passed one of our vehicles onto Jeff, and we knew we didn't have another vehicle to give to Doug when it was his turn to start driving. So I made the call. And sure enough, it was for real. And the car was given to Doug at the perfect time because he was already working part-time as a graphic designer while in high school.

The car was a Chevy Beretta that ran well with no rust, and because the color was faded—basically, nonexistent in a few places—the only thing needed would be a paint job. So for six hundred dollars at Maaco, Doug's car got a new paint job and was ready for him when got his permit at sixteen. What a great blessing. A need was met, and Doug learned a valuable lesson.

After reading the previous sections, some will be tempted to scoff at these traditional views and say, "He's just old fashioned." My response to that is this: God has never changed. He is the same yesterday, today and forever. You will never go wrong in honoring God and putting Him first.

This is about ownership. Who owns you? Who owns your time, your talents and your treasures? God already owns it all and can take it away at any time. Even the very breath we breathe He holds in the palm of His hand. The sad fact is that a majority of people are either ignorant of this concept or choose to ignore it.

Some will say I'm over the top in my beliefs, but I say I'm just Biblical. To the thousands of people who have met me, you know who I am and you know my life.

Christ told us in Matthew 7:13-14, "Enter ye into the straight gate for wide is the gate and broad is the way that leadeth to destruction and many there be which go in there at. Because straight is the gate and narrow is the way which leadeth unto life and *few* there be that find it." Verse 21 of the same chapter says, "Not everyone that sayeth unto me 'Lord, Lord,' shall enter into the kingdom of Heaven, but he that doeth the will of my Father, which is in Heaven." We can never be too careful. Furthermore, Matthew 6:34 says, "Seek ye first the Kingdom of God and His righteousness and all these things will be added unto you." More important than anything this world has to offer, we wanted our kids to understand the value of this lesson.

I always refer to my wife, Trish, as the glue that holds the family together. She travels with the group most of the time but usually works behind the scenes, out of the limelight, never on stage, just holding the fort together. Through her prayers, our family was restored. I could not do what I do without her, and I would not be where I am today without her at my side.

During recent years, Trish has been struggling with Grave's disease, which affects the thyroid. Many people who are familiar with our ministry are not aware of this. However, Trish has faced this problem with the same poise and grace with which she has faced every other challenge in life, going from hyper-thyroidism, where she experienced tremors, hair loss, and skin complications, to the extreme of hypo-thyroidism, experiencing extreme tiredness, cold, and depression, just to name a few of the symptoms.

This has not been an easy road to travel, but I love her just the same, and I am confident that God will bring her through this, just as he has brought our family through every other situation. As we look to the future, I am looking forward to spending time with Trish and our new grandson and any other grandchildren that we may be blessed with in the future.

Trish has often questioned her value and contribution to years of ministry. But recently, I shared with her that I often hear people say that when Trish walks into a room, she brings a calming effect to those around her. Her opinions are valued, and people often comment on the way she respects her husband and fills her role in ministry. When the writer of Proverbs said, "Who can find a virtuous woman?" I'd like to think he was writing about Trish.

I am embracing the change that is coming and am eagerly waiting to see what the next chapter of life will hold. When I think about everything that's happened, it's surreal. I've even pinched myself a few times and said, "Has this really happened to me?"

Yes, I've suffered through horrific pain and have bullied my way down roads no man ought to ever travel. I should have been dead several times, imprisoned, or left out on the streets as a broken, ruined man. Those are the rewards I heartily sought after.

But… *God changed me.* He had other plans for my life and restored and healed our family. I don't know if you can appreciate what I'm saying, but understand this—God's power *is* truly awesome. I'm amazed that God is using our story and our songs to reach out to thousands of others just as desperate as I was.

If there is anything that we have learned, it's that God always takes care of His children. It's a God thing. We are living the reality of the song,

"His Eye is on the Sparrow." His eyes *are* watching us, and as our faith increases, God continues to bless.

He has allowed me to live the dream of being in ministry with my family. Together, we are one. What we do is make music together. While riding in the truck with Doug recently, I said, "Doug, we can't let the music die. That's what makes us who we are. Let's determine that wherever the long road takes us, we will make music together."

CHAPTER 25

Excuse Me?

Well, I thought we were at the end. However, the long road has taken yet another twist and there is more to tell.

Since late September 2008, when we originally planned the conclusion of this story, it's been as though the inspiration faucet turned off. I just couldn't get any more words to flow. Writing the previous chapters was therapeutic, allowing an avenue of venting and giving praise. For various reasons—three weddings in less than two years (my kids), the wedding of my editor, and a funeral (sadly, Dad's)—several years have elapsed since the last chapter.

Shortly after the death of my father, I sensed the Holy Spirit allowing my creative side and inspiration to return. My co-author, Burton Cole, and I spent many long hours marathoning to update all of the previous chapters.

As Paul Harvey would say, "And now, the *rest* of the story."

In the summer of 2008, we received a call to book a concert at Reash United Brethren Church in Cochranton, Pennsylvania. A man by the name of Jesse Arnett scheduled us to sing there in October.

During the course of several conversations, Jesse mentioned that they were losing their pastor who had been there for fifteen years. Call me crazy, but at that very moment it was as if the Holy Spirit tapped me and said, "Randy, you ought to consider being their pastor." I immediately brushed the thought aside as ridiculous.

We played the concert at Reash Church, and I met the outgoing pastor, a good man. Once again, the Holy Spirit tapped me and said, "Randy, you ought to consider being their pastor." And just as quickly as the thought came, I brushed it aside and said, "Lord, I am not preacher material, no way, no how, not ever. I'm a singer, not a preacher."

Several weeks passed and we were in the heavy part of our Christmas concert schedule Out of the blue, Jesse called again. He knew I was well-connected in ministry and thought I might know of someone who could fill in while they searched for a new pastor. I gave Jesse a couple of names to consider, and I also mentioned that on occasion I had filled in for a Sunday or two for pastors who needed a weekend off. And our conversation ended.

Once again, the Holy Spirit tapped me and said, "Randy, you ought to consider being their pastor."

And I said, "No, Lord, I am not a preacher."

During that time, Jesse would often arrive in my driveway unannounced, just to talk to me. Every time I saw that gray Dodge, I was thinking, "Please, Lord, not again."

Around Christmastime 2008, Jesse called *again*, just like a bad dream with no end. "You mentioned that you've filled in at a few places. Would you be able to help us in January?" I checked my schedule, and sure enough I was free on the 4th and the 25th. I had to do something to get this guy off my back.

The Holy Spirit immediately mentioned to me, "Randy, you ought to consider being their pastor." And I said, "Lord, that's the most ridiculous, absurd thought that's ever been in my mind. I am not preacher material."

On Sunday morning, January 4, 2009, on my way to fill in at Reash Church, somehow, way down in the depths of my soul, I knew that my life was changing. And I knew that Reash Church was going to be a part of it.

Trish knew that I had been struggling with something as I was not sleeping well at night. "Whatever your deal is, whatever you're going through, you need to get it resolved because *I'm* not getting any sleep at night." I still hadn't told her what was going on in my head and the thoughts that the Holy Spirit had kept in the forefront of my mind. I was being called into the ministry and was too stubborn to give in.

I filled in again on the 25th and this only intensified the feelings that were in my heart. Bear in mind that on both of these Sundays, their attendance was only sixteen people. By now with our music ministry, I was used to singing to a *much* larger crowd. On Christmas Sunday 2008, the attendance at Reash Church was only *seven*. No one in his right mind would want to become the pastor of this church.

Finally, in February, I explained to my doctor that I was having trouble sleeping. His diagnosis: "You're in your early forties. Life is changing. You're probably dealing with some mild anxiety and depression. I can give you something to help take the edge off."

I took the medication for four days and faced the reality that I knew deep down in my heart the root of my real problem. God was calling me to pastor at Reash Church. The medication was never going to help and was quickly discarded. It was one doctor's feeble attempt at prescribing a medical solution to a spiritual problem.

In mid-February, I finally made the call that initiated major change. Instead of Jesse calling me, this time I called him. "Jess, this is the most absurd, ridiculous thing that I've ever done, and I am questioning my sanity. But I believe that the Holy Spirit is directing me to throw my hat into the ring for consideration as your new pastor."

Jesse was elated. He told me that four of the people from the church had been meeting on Monday nights, praying that God would lay it on the heart of the right man to come and be their pastor.

I immediately had peace because I had finally been obedient and could feel the weight rolling off my shoulders. I was now willing. The rest would be in God's hands.

Before I hung up, Jesse threw me a curve. Another man had contacted them just the day before and said he would be willing to be their pastor. I said, "Jesse, if he's the one you choose, then I'm free." I added, "I'm going to pray that he's your man." *And I'd be off the hook.* The rest is history. After meeting with the remnant of the congregation that was left and agreeing to candidate officially, I put out a fleece. When it came up for voting, anything less than a unanimous vote would be a sign that I should not go.

The vote was taken. It was unanimous, and the ball was now in my court. Trish and I began serving on March 1, 2009, with twenty-two in attendance for my first official Sunday.

I knew the road was not going to be easy. The church was struggling due to misunderstandings and doctrinal disagreements, resulting in a congregation of almost seventy people dwindling to nearly nothing. Wounds needed healing. In order for the church to recover, we would need a new vision, new direction, reinforced spiritual foundation, and construction of a new infrastructure. This would be like a new church plant, beginning at ground zero.

So there I was, a guy with no formal Bible training, green as the grass. The only tools in my tool bag were years of management and administrative experience. I had been around churches all my life and had completed several years in music ministry. I had some basic ideas of where we could start. It was overwhelming, but I couldn't let the church leadership see my weakness. When I was around the people from the church, I had to present an air of confidence. My management training had taught me that in tense situations, you never let them see you sweat.

All I could do was throw myself fully on the mercy of God. "God, I don't have a clue. I don't know where to start or what to do first. You're going to have to show me."

A few months into pastoring, while interviewing with the IFBC (International Fellowship of Bible Churches) to receive my credentials, I shared with them some of the changes I made at the church, like dissolving their old church board and electing a new one, and implementing a whole new leadership structure. They told me, "Randy, you're going to fit in well here. So far, you've done it all wrong."

All I could rely on was good old common sense, years of experience in music ministry and business, and most importantly, the leadership of the Holy Spirit. I now found myself praying for three things—wisdom, guidance and patience.

Over the years, God has gifted me with an outgoing personality and the ability to relate to people. I love people, and I love being around them. I like to find out what they do and often find myself analyzing them to determine what makes them tick.

After arming myself with business cards, it was off to knocking on doors introducing myself to the community, meeting with the church members and anyone else who would have me. When I got to a house and someone would say, "Well, we go to another church up the road," my response was, "That's great. However, I'm the new pastor, and I just want to put a face with the name. And if I can help in any way, you let me know. If you're already attending another church, then you need to stay committed to the church you attend and go to a place where you're being fed spiritually."

As time went on, we began tracking the numbers. Eight for Sunday school. Thirty-two for worship. Sunday after Sunday, our numbers grew. Thirty-two. Forty-three. Fifty. On our first Easter, we were in the seventies. And still it continued. Eighties. Nineties. Then one Sunday morning, we hit that thrilling number of one hundred.

During this time, the Spirit of God was moving. The altar was busy. Various people were praying and receiving Christ. Some came for rededication, and others prayed for their families. After about two years, we were consistently running in the high eighties or nineties most Sunday mornings. Sunday school attendance had grown and was now in the thirties and forties. One exciting thing was that the attendance of our Wednesday night prayer and Bible study was also growing. We were now consistently in the thirties and forties.

As for me, I just kept doing the only thing I knew to do—loving the people and preaching it straight.

I consider myself to be somewhat animated. Recently Jesse joked as we were installing closed-circuit TV for our nursery staff, "What good's it going to do if we can't get our pastor to stay behind the pulpit when he's preaching?" I told him that's what they make a wide angle for. I like to move around a lot when I'm preaching, and people usually don't fall asleep during service.

The journey has been phenomenal so far. As I look back, I am thankful that I was obedient. Our church is filled every Sunday with some of the greatest people in the world. We are a family, and we love each other.

Since the journey began on March 1, 2009, here is a brief summary of some of the things that have happened:

We are now independent and our name has changed to Reash Community Church. We have outgrown a building that was comfortable for ninety to ninety-five, added an assistant pastor, and our average worship attendance is between one hundred thirty to one hundred sixty people each morning. As I write this, we just finished one hundred twenty-two consecutive weeks of one hundred or more worshippers in attendance each Sunday, with our high being one hundred seventy-four and our low one hundred.

Just recently, we opened an upstairs classroom for a balcony to make room for about twenty-five more people. Our Sunday school attendance averages around seventy-five. We now have a teen class and a young adult class, both running in the double digits. Wednesday nights have been my greatest joy. For nearly the past year, we have been running in the sixties and seventies, with our highest attendance at eighty-five.

Our Wednesday night crowd is the backbone of our church, and it's the most important service of our week. The altar continues to be busy; lives are being changed; and we are seeing the hand of God moving.

I'll never forget the look on Betty's face when, after several months of attending services, she came to the altar one morning. After praying the sinner's prayer with tears streaming and a new look on her face, she sighed and said, "Oh, I've wanted to do this for a long time."

Just a few Sundays ago, after I preached a message on 1 Peter 5:8, one man nearly ran to the altar, and another woman came weeping, which prompted several others to step out. Some came for salvation. Others were coming for rededication.

You're probably thinking that I'm a numbers-driven pastor. Nothing could be farther from the truth. Large numbers never impress me, but spiritual depth excites me. I have seen too many churches that have grown wide, but have never grown deep roots. I have often raised this concern with the church leaders, that our emphasis must be on reinforcing our spiritual foundation, and God will take care of the numbers.

The vision of our church is to see people saved, encouraged, discipled, and brought to a place of surrender and sacrifice, so they, in turn, can go out and win others. It's called duplication.

Due to a continued growth pattern, we were able to purchase nearly seven acres of property along U.S. Route 19, about 3 miles from our current location, which we are developing to build a larger sanctuary.

A note of praise: The property is paid for, and over the past couple of years, nearly all the property has been cleared, five loads of logs were harvested, the driveway has been put in, septic system has been approved, and we are hoping to be able to break ground in the very near future.

Along with this God has been blessing in the area of our giving as we have seen a tremendous increase of funds as a direct result of a tithing to missions program that was implemented in the past 18 months.

On a couple of occasions, we have been blessed by some wonderful people who do not attend our church who have contributed $20,000 to our efforts, a definite sign of God's approval that we are on the right track.

One thing I know for sure. In spite of all my failures, God is on the move, and He is rewarding the faithfulness and obedience of His servants.

As for Trish and me, we're still doing what we do—loving on the people and preaching it straight. Since becoming the pastor, I've done many things I never did before. My philosophy is that I'm willing to do anything to help people in the church, so long as I do not compromise my personal views or convictions. I do not want to offend my Lord.

I've laid block for a pump house. I've picked rocks out of a field. Twice, we organized work crews to help a family clean up after a devastating fire in the community. We've helped people move. And since God blessed me with a small backhoe, I have dug many ditches and have not been afraid to get my hands dirty. Just recently, I jokingly told one of my church members that I was a preacher on Sunday and a ditch-digger on Monday. We laughed, but that's the truth. My work at the church involves the wearing of many hats and my feeble attempts to do things I've never done before.

On Saturday nights, you can find me at the church preparing for Sunday morning, but on other days you might find me on the backhoe digging stumps out of the property we are developing for building our new church. The constant theme on my mind is, let's get 'er done one way or another, whatever it takes to see souls brought into the Kingdom, so long as we don't compromise in the process. Thinking outside the box is a good thing.

When we were discussing the possibility of building a new church, my statement was, "If we hold onto this old building just for sentimental reasons or look on it as the golden calf, we will never grow. We have to allow God to change the way we think, so we can become what He wants us to be."

Sometimes that means we have to think outside the box. It's amazing how tradition can stunt the growth of a church.

Maybe you're thinking, "Man, this preacher walks on water. Look at all the great things that have happened." Have you ever heard the statement, "He failed his way to success"? That's me. I assure you that I am about the most imperfect creature God has ever made. I pray every day, "Lord, whatever challenges come today, please help me not to mess up."

Every day there's something new. Six-thirty in the morning, the telephone rings, and the day I thought was planned is now changed. There are weddings to prepare for, funerals to conduct, pastoral counseling for married couples, financial advice. I've even had phone calls asking if I had seen the weather forecast.

During the past three years, I completed the requirements for Ordination at Northeast Ohio Bible Institute, and on September 16, 2012, I was officially ordained through the International Fellowship of Bible Churches (IFBC).

During the ordination service, Dr. William Sillings, our conference president said, "People don't care how much you know until they know how much you care." That statement really struck a chord in me, and I pray that I will always live up to that statement. My ordination was a great night, a humbling night, and one I will never forget. It was just another milestone on the long road.

I have been praying that God will send a revival to our area. In the process of praying, He has pointed out areas in my life where I need to grow, things that need to change. I have been asking the Lord to bend me low, to break me and allow the revival to begin with me.

I believe that if the members of our church can catch the vision of self-sacrifice, self-examination, and allow ourselves to be brought low, a phenomenal revival will sweep our area, and God will receive all the glory.

Several in the community had written "Ichabod" over the door—a phrase from I Samuel that often refers to the glory having departed from a church—and said that the church was dead. However, as God breathed new life into the valley of dry bones, He has done the same at our church. A church that was in drastic need of healing and restoration is now alive and well.

I tell my people often, our best is yet to come. When it happens, we will all be able to stand back and say, "Look what God has done in this place. Who of you are willing to stand and go with me?"

I love the people. They are my spiritual family, and together we have stormed the gates. We've prayed together and cried together, and wherever this journey ends, we're traveling together.

CHAPTER 26

The Last Three Weeks

As we write this final chapter, I find myself with Burton at the Warren-Trumbull County Public Library in Warren, Ohio. Much effort has already gone into this project. And yet, as we sit here, I realize that there are still many things that need to be told.

The road from the beginning to this point has been long—filled with twists and turns, bumps and potholes. I have grown over the years. I have tried to be like a sponge and absorb and learn as much as I could about God, about life, and about what really matters. I'm reminded of the poem by Robert Frost, "The Road Not Taken," which talks about two roads that diverged in a yellow wood. Two clear choices stood out. One road was heavily traveled, and the other was less traveled.

The night of August 18 of 1993, I stood at that crossroads. I could follow the path of least resistance, which would be the easy way, or I could accept the narrow way that would be filled with many unknowns and struggles. But that night, I chose "*. . . the one less traveled by / And that has made all the difference.*"

I have shared many details about my mother and dad. I am confident and happy to say that in spite of all of our past dysfunction, my mother is a different woman today. Just as I am not the man I used to be, my mother is not the woman she used to be. When I visit her or talk to her on the phone, I often hear her tell me that she prays for me and my family every day. I hear her talking about having her devotions every morning and reading her Bible. Over the years, I have seen a change in my mother, and I believe she is endeavoring to do her best to serve the Lord with all of her heart.

In spite of all the pain, misunderstandings, and challenges of the past, my dad said, "In the end, we're going to be winners." When he was first diagnosed with bone cancer, he told me, "I can see a clear road to the end. For my family and for your mother, I choose to fight this as long as I can. It's a beautiful thing to realize after what we've been through as a family, that in the end, it's all coming together and I'm a winner."

And he would say, "We're a winner, son."

One time, a friend of mine who was in the tour business asked if I could drive him and his wife to New York City for the American Bus Association Convention. I agreed and also received permission to take my dad along with me. Dad had never spent much time in New York City, so this would be a great time for us to be together. I would also be able to learn about the city to help with my own tours. That day, I had the rare opportunity to have a deep conversation with my dad. There were things about his life that were a mystery, and while sitting at a McDonald's restaurant at Tenth and Thirty-Fourth Streets, I asked Dad, "Why did you marry my mother?"

"Son, I was in the car at a crossroads just outside Dayton, Pennsylvania, not far from the farmhouse where your mother lived. I had a choice to make. Do I turn and cross the tracks and go down to be with your mother, or do I go north, near East Springfield, Pennsylvania, to another girl that I liked? Rather than the long road, I took the short one, and the rest is history."

He told me there were things about his life that he would never tell anyone, mental hang-ups that he would carry with him to his grave. He said, "Looking back, marrying your mother was one of the best things that happened to me, because in spite of all of our disagreements and battles, your mother helped keep me on the straight and narrow."

I remember wondering, "Did they love each other, or were they just old school and committed to staying together no matter what?" This I know, over the nearly fifty-seven years they were married a true love grew between them, and after we kids were gone, in their crippled way, while also carrying the baggage of the past, their love grew.

If you were to ask me if I have any regrets in life, one of those would be that if I could do one thing over, I would make sure that I spent more time with my dad. He was a complicated man. When he believed in something, he believed in it the most radical way he could.

He was convinced that the King James Version of the Bible, published in 1611, was the only version of the Bible ever needed, or for that matter, the only version that should ever be spoken of. In his mind, anything other than this would be compromise. He vigorously defended his position till the day he drew his last breath.

In the beginning of 2011, Dad purchased and proudly wore a pin that celebrated the 400th anniversary of the 1611 King James Version. I felt it only proper that we allow him to wear that pin during calling hours at the funeral home, as it was such a part of him. As we were tucking Dad in before the casket was closed, we removed that pin. I carry it in my left jacket pocket every Sunday when I'm preaching, just a little bit of Dad with me.

But don't get me wrong. We did get to spend some time together. Trucking was part of Dad's life, and after he was retired and no longer able to drive, I took him along with me as I was driving part-time trying to make ends meet. On one of those days, he was riding as I was driving a tri-axle dump truck from Stoneboro to Ellwood City, round after round, back and forth. Dad loved it. He was glad I had my commercial driver's license, and I was glad he could ride along.

While going up a big hill, Dad was critiquing my shifting. "C'mon, son, you're working this Mack truck too hard. You're lugging the engine too hard, and therefore, you're losing your power. The next time we come down here, I want you to downshift when I tell you, and if you do that, you'll walk right up over this hill."

Well, the next trip came. Dad said, "Don't watch your tachometer but, rather listen for the sound of the engine." He was an ace. I followed his advice and from then on, we were eating the hills alive! Dad may not have known much about other things, but he knew trucks, and he was an expert at handling them.

Later, when I graduated to tractor-trailer rigs, I had the opportunity to have Dad in the truck a few times. When we were in the yard getting loaded, I would often let Dad move the truck, and when the Jake brake would bark, he would say, "Ah, that's music to my ears."

Even though Dad was battling cancer, he still had the hope that someday he could buy an old 1960s series B Model Mack. He would often say, "Son, if you want to be a real truck driver, you learn to drive a B Model Mack without power steering and two gearshifts." That's what he started with.

Dad had said that he wanted to make it to his eightieth birthday. The kids and I had one of the best nights ever with him as we honored him on November 16, 2010. I bought him a new Navy hat, as he was a Navy veteran, and Trish and I bought him a toy tractor-trailer rig that had the word "Navy" and a picture of a large aircraft carrier on the side of the trailer. Dad was proud of the fact that he had served on the USS *Antietam* during the Korean War. It was the first aircraft carrier that had a side catapult for fighter jets to take off. He was a seaman and would often refer to himself as, "just a dumb seaman."

Throughout the three years of his illness, due to the distance between our homes and difficulty in communicating, Dad regretfully faced this disease mostly alone, except for Mom at his side. We knew he was fighting it and doing everything he could to survive. But his cancer made him highly susceptible to pneumonia. There were times when I talked to him on the phone that I could sense he was laboring with his breathing. I said, "Dad, you need to get to the emergency room."

About two years before he was diagnosed with cancer, Dad had a severe urinary tract infection and nearly lost his life as a result of septic shock. Mom found him in bad shape, lying on the basement floor. In my mind, this was the beginning of an ultimate end, as later he was diagnosed with his cancer.

When Dad would take a bad spell, Mom would call me. I'd be off running to Armstrong County Memorial Hospital to make sure he would be taken care of. This happened several times.

Then, on February 17, 2011, I received a phone call from my mother, who said Dad was not breathing right. I told her, "You need to get him to the emergency room." The doctors had already told him that if he waited past the first twenty-four hours of the symptoms, he probably would not make it. It was always Dad's nature to push things to the "Nth" degree, but Mom convinced him to go, only for him to be sent back home with heavy antibiotics.

I'm not sure what Dad went through the next two days. But what he described to me was that he couldn't sleep at all and he felt like his skin was crawling, maybe as a result of the medication or something. He said it felt like things were closing in.

Then again on Saturday afternoon, the 19th, my mother called. "Dad is not getting any better."

I told her, "You've got to get him to the emergency room."

When I got to the hospital that night, I knew my dad was in bad shape. He was in congestive heart failure, clearly in distress. A noted difference this time was that his stomach was distended, which I had never observed before. The very strong medicine he had been taking for his bone cancer had finally taken its toll, and he was going into heart, lung, and kidney failure.

As he lay in the emergency room that night, just as I'd had the premonition about my sister and her passing, I had a feeling that Dad would never leave the hospital.

I learned more about my dad in the last three weeks of his life than I did in all the years I lived at home with him and even after I was married. His eyes were blue, and they twinkled when he smiled. He had spunk and an inner-strength that wouldn't quit.

After the first week in the hospital, we could clearly see that Dad was progressively getting worse. Yet through it all, he maintained a positive attitude. He was facing open-heart surgery which was the only possible way that he could survive. However, they had to get the pneumonia cleared up enough for him to handle the breathing machine.

I helped my dad stand in front of the mirror in the hospital room to shave. I don't know if I'd ever noticed it before, but this day I saw his frailty. As he shaved, I reminded him of the times when, as a little boy I used to watch him shave. Now, he was barely able to do it by himself.

Dad was a stickler for keeping his hair short, but had been unable to go to the barber's to get it cut. Knowing that he probably would never leave the hospital, I contacted his barber, Fred Clark, and asked if he would be willing to come to the hospital and cut Dad's hair. Fred agreed, and Dad told me, "Son, you're Johnny-on-the-spot. Not much gets past you." He was so thankful that Fred came and cut his hair.

In spite of all of the differences we had and all the pain of the past, God put a love in my heart for my dad, and I wanted to do everything I could do to make him as comfortable as possible during this time. He loved having the family together, and during his last three weeks, he was most happy when everyone was in his room. The more the merrier.

In his later years, for some reason I became the spiritual leader in the family. Dad had me pray for family get-togethers and on holidays. This night, there we were, the whole family together in Dad's room. He loved it. We all joined hands and we prayed for Dad, that God's will would be accomplished in the days that lay ahead.

He would soon be transferred to Butler Memorial Hospital for the open-heart surgery. By now, my sister Carol and I were taking turns being at Dad's side and trying to see that Mom was taken care of at home. It's amazing how during these sorts of times, families come together for the common good of one.

On the last night before Dad took a real downward turn, I had to be back home for business at the church. But I then made the seventy-five-mile trip back to the hospital to pull an all-nighter with Dad. When I got there, he was in severe distress, and the medical staff made the decision to put him into intensive care. I was not allowed to be in with Dad that night, which meant a long night in the waiting room.

When morning came, they allowed me to go in and see him. By now, the rest of the family was there, too, as we were making preparations to transfer him by ambulance to Butler Memorial Hospital. Carol and I knew that Dad still had important papers that he needed to sign to take care of some end-of-life issues. That morning, without any hesitation, Dad signed every one of them.

On one of my rotations in his room, I knelt on the floor beside Dad's bed. I held his hand in the same fashion that someone would give a "high five." Neither Dad nor I could say anything for a period of time. All we did was look at each other.

Finally, he pointed to me and said, "I see it in your eyes, Son." Both he and I knew that the time for passing the torch had come. The time for him to move on had arrived, and the time for me to step up and take my role was soon coming. We always know these days will happen, but we're never prepared for them when they do.

We took pictures of him on that day—He and Carol, He and I, Mom and Dad—any memories we could get. Later that afternoon, Dad was transferred to Butler.

Right now, I think I should digress and tell you that almost a year before his death, while visiting him at his home in Worthington, Dad handed me an envelope. I keep it today as one of my most treasured possessions.

Written on the outside of it were the words, "My testimony—Dan E. Tarr Keeling." Inside was his attempt at writing poetry, a poem he titled, *Daddy's Pocket*. After I read it, he told me, "Son, you might be able to make a song about this someday."

At the age of seventy-nine, Dad still had a longing to have a relationship with a real dad. He still wanted to experience what it felt like to have the love of a real father. I think Dad had been on a quest to find this his entire life.

He told me of an incident that he observed while pumping gas at the Exxon station in Butler. A car pulled into the parking lot, and out of the driver's side stepped a big man. This man was a man's man, Dad said. Out of the other side of the car bounded a little boy about the age of three. Dad watched as the little boy walked around the front of the vehicle. He calmly and confidently reached up and put his hand in his daddy's pocket, and together they walked across the parking lot into the station. Dad said the big man didn't try to hurry. He walked the same pace as the little boy.

Something about this scene struck my father. "I am just like that little boy. And that big man is just like God. And as long as I keep my hand in Daddy's pocket, I'm going to make it."

As he later wrote in the poem, "My Daddy is bigger than all the other daddies combined, and with one step He can span the whole universe. Oh, how I love my Daddy and my Daddy loves me. How do I know this? Because He told me."

Somehow this scene awakened the innocent little Dan E. Tarr Keeling that had been searching for a real dad. His quest was over. God was his Daddy, and he was his Daddy's son.

Many times during those final three weeks, Carol and I reminded him, "Dad, don't forget, just keep your hand in Daddy's pocket," and he would respond with a thumbs up.

Dad was never able to have the open-heart surgery that he desperately needed, and with each passing day, he progressively worsened. On the Sunday before Dad passed away, after taking care of my duties at the church, I traveled back to spend the night with him at the hospital.

By now, Dad's blood oxygen saturation levels were too low, and they put him on a bi-pap machine, which constantly forced air into his lungs. The only way I can describe what this machine feels like would be to stick your head out of a jet plane traveling at Mach 2. All night long, Dad turned and tossed. "I have to have some relief. I have to have some relief."

I rubbed his back and tried to make him comfortable, as Dad loved human touch. I also asked him if he wanted me to read the Bible to him, and he said yes. I was so tired that I couldn't see straight, and I can't remember anything I read to him that night, but I knew he enjoyed it. I was nearly frazzled and real glad when Carol came in the morning to relieve me. I am so thankful for my sister's faithfulness during this time. I also have to give mention to Rev. James Lynn and Rev. Bill Fish for being faithful to the family and to my father.

During the coming days, Dad went from the bi-pap to being intubated and placed on a respirator. An external heart pump was inserted, and he was placed in a medically induced coma. For most of two days, we were not able to communicate with him. On top of all this, his kidneys began to fail. My sister and I had already had discussions with Dad about his wishes concerning being placed on life support if he got to the place where there was no quality of life. Dad said if there was something that could be done to save his life, he was willing to go through it if there was a reasonable chance for a positive outcome.

On Saturday, March 12, 2011, they woke Dad and gave the family an opportunity to communicate with him. He still couldn't talk due to the tubes, but we had taught him to communicate by blinking his eyes. Three blinks were "I love you." With a twinkle in his eye, he winked at all the girls of the family. Somehow in spite of all of his pain, he still had that boyhood spunk. My sister was elated when he winked at her.

Throughout that day, one by one, all the grandkids and everyone who was there had an opportunity to spend time with Dad. We would talk to him, then blink three times at him, and he would blink back.

By late afternoon, we received confirmation from the medical staff that the inevitable was going to happen and that there was no hope. We had exhausted every option. I knew it was time to have a conversation with Dad. Kneeling beside his bed once again, I asked him, "Have you had enough, Dad? Are you ready to get all this off of you?" And he nodded his head yes. My sister asked him the same thing, and he nodded.

I asked Dad if he wanted me to read some Scripture to him, and he nodded yes. One of his favorite psalms was Psalm 27. I had read it to him before, but this time it took on new meaning. "The Lord is my light and my salvation. Whom shall I fear? The Lord is the strength of my life. Of whom shall I be afraid?" I often wondered why Dad loved this psalm. But this day, as I read to him, verse 10 stood out: "When my father and my mother forsake me, then the Lord will take me." His real mother died when he was three days old. His real father gave him away. And now his hand was in his Heavenly Daddy's pocket.

After finishing this psalm, I asked Dad if he would like me to read more, and he nodded. I said, "Psalm 23?" He nodded yes. When I got to the sixth verse, I said the words, "Surely goodness and mercy shall follow me all the days of my life and I," and I pointed to him and touched him, "Dan Keeling, will dwell in the house of the Lord forever. Amen." Out of the left side of his lips, I could see my dad feebly attempting to say, "Amen."

Throughout the early evening, with the permission of the family, they began removing all the life-support machines. And with him fully in his right mind, full well knowing that his time to depart was at hand, we made the choice to make him as comfortable as possible. He wanted the tube removed, and other than some medication to help his blood pressure, a special oxygen mask was applied, and the next hour and a half I will never forget. Each one of us said our goodbyes again. Dad couldn't move his hands, but he could nod his head. I had positioned myself at the foot of his bed so I could look him in the eye, and I would say, "Dad, are you okay?" I would show the thumbs up, and he would nod, "Yes."

The preachers were there. All the grandkids were there. My sister and her husband, my niece and nephew—everyone was in the room.

Uncle Paul Troup and Aunt Carol were there. My mother's brother Uncle Paul and my dad were very close and treated each other like brothers. I remember Uncle Paul saying to my dad that night, "Dan, you know if they take this tube out, you're going to meet your Maker." Uncle Paul wanted to make sure that Dad knew what he was facing. But Dad nodded that he understood.

I have great respect for Uncle Paul as he faithfully served in the United States Army during the Vietnam War. In fact, every one of Mom's brothers served in the military with the exception of Uncle Gary.

Sometimes when I think of the drama of the moment, it is overwhelming. Dad loved our singing. One night earlier in the week, we had permission from the hospital staff to sing for Dad, and he loved it. On that final Saturday night, I said to the family, "Somehow I just feel like we need to sing." And for the next forty-five minutes, with everyone standing around his bed, we sang "Amazing Grace," "Great is Thy Faithfulness," "It Will be Worth it All," and many others. At the end of each song, I would look at Dad and say, "Dad, do you want us to sing more?" And he would nod his head yes.

In my mind, I would like to believe that as Dad was hearing our voices blended together, he could also hear a Heavenly choir singing in the distance, one that was calling him Home. His coronation day was about to begin. A young boy from Mingo Junction, Ohio, who lived most of his childhood in Wellsburg, West Virginia; a boy who had a touch of a Southern accent and would say "gnarl" instead of "narrow," and "chury" instead of "cherry;" a boy who never had much and worked hard for everything he had, was going home a prince. He was a child of the King.

When we were through singing and after more prayer, the nurses asked us to step out, as they could see Dad was in more distress. About ten minutes later, they called us back in and by then, the light of his eyes was fading. I was standing on the left side of his bed, right near his head, and I told him, "Dad, we're here. We're with you. We're not going to leave you. It's okay to go. It's okay to go. Connie's waiting on you, Dad." And I promised him that I would see him again.

By now, tears flowed freely from everyone in the room. We were watching the clock, and shortly before 9:00 p.m., Dad left this life a winner. He had won the race. He had finished the course. He had fought the good fight. His long road had come to an end.

After the funeral service, we had a private graveside gathering for the immediate family at Mount Zion Cemetery. The locals know the area as Beautiful Lookout. We instructed the funeral director that we were going to stay until they lowered Dad's casket into the ground. I'd promised Dad that I would stay with him till the end, and this was still part of it.

As they tried lowering the vault into the ground, we realized that the hole had been dug just a little too "gnarl," as Dad would say. And so there we were, standing by Dad's grave, trying to push and pry on the vault. I'm not sure who said it, but I think it was my sister who made the observation that even his burial was complicated. Very fitting for a complicated man who did everything the hard way!

Of all the funerals that I have officiated, my dad's was the easiest. God gave me an unusual confidence that day, and I wanted to do my dad proud. No one could speak for him better than one of his own. It was a privilege for me to conduct Dad's service. The kids and I sang "I Rest My Case at the Cross," which Dad had requested for his funeral, and my nephew Rick played "He Looked Beyond My Fault and Saw My Need," which is to the tune of "Danny Boy," on the violin. It was a beautiful service, complete with military honors, the firing of a twenty-one-gun salute, and a flag-folding ceremony by a special honor guard from Fort Indian Town Gap, Pennsylvania. I carry one of the shell casings from Dad's twenty-one gun-salute in my right suit coat pocket, just another way to remember my father.

Of all the many things I didn't know about my dad, there are some things that I know for sure. In the end, he loved Jesus. He loved his God. He loved his wife and his kids. He loved anything he could read about Abraham Lincoln. He loved his country. And he loved music.

Not long after the funeral was over and life was beginning to return to normal, my inspiration to write returned. One afternoon while looking at Dad's poem, "Daddy's Pocket," the tune and the words began to flow.

I saw it just the other day
A little boy and his dad
He was only three years old
Daddy was a big, strong man

Side by side they were walking
Across the parking lot
Daddy leaned over
And I heard him say
These words from the heart

(chorus)
"Put your hand into my pocket
As we walk along today
I don't want to see you hurt
I love you more than words can say
Hold on tight
Don't let go
I'll be right here by your side
Keep your hand in Daddy's pocket
And everything will be all right."

"My Daddy's bigger than all
The other dads combined
He can span the mighty universe
With just a single stride
When I'm walking through the valley
And fear grips my heart
Daddy leans over
And I hear him say
These words from the heart

(repeat chorus)

(bridge)
Now I know that there are many kids
Who never had a dad
Or daddy was just too busy
Pursuing other plans
But there's a God who really cares
A God who understands
Put your hand into His pocket
Put your hand in Daddy's pocket

I saw it just the other day
A little boy and his dad...

Shortly after we released the single of "Daddy's Pocket" in November of 2011, I made a trip to the cemetery and placed two copies of the CD on Dad's grave. And each time I have visited the grave since then, I have replaced the copies of "Daddy's Pocket." As long as I live, each time that I visit Dad's grave, I will always leave a copy. My daddy was a hero, and I want the people who may pass by his grave to know that he was loved and will never be forgotten.

Today, if you were to travel to Beautiful Lookout and view my dad's tombstone, you would see two words inscribed there. These were words of great meaning to Dad: "Mercy" and "Hope."

In summation, where would any of us be without mercy and hope? To think that God loves us so much that He would be willing to take *my* place and *your* place on Calvary, taking the punishment that we deserved upon Himself—this is difficult to comprehend. But because of what He did, we have hope: hope of eternal life, hope of freedom in Christ, hope that we can be changed and have victory over sin.

Now as a pastor, if I had only one message to preach, it would be that every one of us is traveling somewhere. As I see it, there are two clear choices. On one hand, the narrow, difficult road leads to the Promised Land. On the other, the broad, easy road leads to destruction. Millions of people are traveling on the easy road unaware that the end is doom.

Every one of us will make a choice. We can choose now to serve Christ or we can choose to ignore Him. One way or another, the Bible says that every knee shall bow, and every tongue shall confess that Jesus Christ is Lord. You can bow now while you still have time, or you can bow later when there is no hope. As long as you are alive and have breath, you still have hope.

Romans 3:23: "For all have sinned and come short of the glory of God."

Romans 6:23: "For the wages of sin is death but the gift of God is eternal life through Jesus Christ our Lord."

Romans 5:8: "But God commendeth his love toward us in that while we were yet sinners, Christ died for us."

1 John 1:9: If we confess our sins, He is faithful and just to forgive us our sins and to cleanse us from all unrighteousness."

II Corinthians 5:17: "Therefore, if any man be in Christ, he is a new creature. Old things are passed away. Behold, all things are become new."

As I write this, please understand that I am a dying man, speaking to men and women who are likewise dying, sharing a message as if it could be my last. I strongly urge you to choose the right road and remember that wherever you are traveling on your own long road, you can always make a U-turn. As long as you are alive, there is always hope and mercy.

As we sing in the second verse of the song "I Know What Lies Ahead":

> *While on this road I get so weary*
> *And often my feet would stray*
> *But a gentle hand still leads me onward*
> *And helps me find my way*
> *As I climb each hill and cross each valley*
> *By His hand I am daily led*
> *But I won't look back*
> *Gonna keep on walkin'*
> *For I know what lies ahead.*

The long road has been hard and difficult, but with my hand in the hand of the One Who can see what's coming around the next bend, I am confident that the long road will take me to the Promised Land.

CPSIA information can be obtained at www.ICGtesting.com
Printed in the USA
BVOW04s1609250314

348707BV00002B/8/P